Guide to Better
Wine and Beer Making
for Beginners

S. M. Tritton
M.P.S., F.R.I.C.

Dover Publications, Inc., New York

by the same author

AMATEUR WINE MAKING

This Dover edition, first published in 1969, is
an unabridged republication of the work originally
published by Faber and Faber Limited in 1965
under the title *Tritton's Guide to Better Wine and
Beer Making for Beginners*.

The present edition, which is for sale in the
United States of America only, contains a special
Note to American Users and a list of American
suppliers of wine-making materials.

Standard Book Number: 486-22528-3
Library of Congress Catalog Card Number: 76-99104

Manufactured in the United States of America
Dover Publications, Inc.
180 Varick Street
New York, N.Y. 10014

Contents

Illustrations

LINE

PLATES

6

Illustrations

TABLES

* *By courtesy of the Brewer's Research Association.*
† *By courtesy of Prof. H. Schanderl, Geisenheim Viticultural Institute, W. Germany.*

7

Note for American Users

When the *Guide to Better Wine and Beer Making* first appeared, the special wine yeasts on which the work in this book was based were difficult to obtain in the U.S.A. Recently, Grey Owl yeasts and other wine-making adjuncts have become easily available; the names of many suppliers are now listed on page 152. Several substitutes for the Grey Owl yeasts are also obtainable, notably a *wine yeast,* Montrachet strain, available as a dry, granular powder in sachets. This yeast ferments well and settles to a firm deposit; only a quarter teaspoonful should be used per gallon of juice. The yeast will keep if stored in a cool dry place. It is obtainable from Scott Laboratories Inc., 860 South 19th Street, Richmond, California 94804. This company also stocks a product called Dextrocheck for testing dry wines for residual sugar content. This is similar to the Clinitest mentioned on page 130.

Campden Tablets (p. 53). Two oz of a 1 per cent solution of sodium metabisulphite can be used instead of the tablet. This is roughly equivalent to 1½ Campden tablets and is prepared by dissolving 1¼ oz of the salt in a U.S. gallon of water.

Yeast Nutrient (p. 51). Diammonium phosphate is a suitable substitute and should be used at the rate of ½ teaspoonful to a gallon of prepared juice.

Yeast Energizers (p. 52) promotes yeast growth through vitamins, biotin and other valuable growth factors and is much more effective than a 100 mgm tablet of vitamin B_1 sometimes advocated instead.

Reductone Tablets (p. 53) contain ascorbic acid and a 500 mgm tablet of vitamin C can be used instead.

8

Note for American Users

Serena Wine Finings (p. 54) are specially formulated to help the amateur in clarifying a wine easily and do not contain bentonite. If the latter or Kieselgur, sold in the U.S.A. as Supercell or Celite, is used then the wine has to be filtered. Add 1½ tablespoonsful of the Kieselgur to one pint of wine and pass this through a fluted filter paper which is supported at the tip with absorbent cotton in a plastic or glass funnel. Pour this wine through the filter and return the filrate till it comes through clear. Stir one tablespoonful of Celite into the remainder of the gallon and continue filtration through the precoated filter. Alternatively, the Kieselgur will settle after 5 to 7 days and the clear wine can be racked off.

Serena Wine Stabilizer (p. 54) contains potassium sorbate which additive is permitted in most wine making countries.

Finally, air locks are also called fermentation traps.

Preface

Winemaking has since olden times been a craft practised by country folk, where it was an admirable way of using up surplus fruit and vegetables. In those days the utensils used were the bread crock, or even the bath tub, and when yeast was required to start the fermentation, baker's yeast was used. With the War years and their sugar rationing, winemaking became an almost forgotten art, but during the last decade wine production by amateurs has taken on enormous proportions and this has been in no little measure stimulated by the publication of many books on wine-making, by the monthly journal *The Amateur Wine Maker*, and by the formation of Wine Circles all over the country.

Although much wine is made domestically there still seems a need to improve wine quality. Making the wine is not enough; a wine has to be nursed to perfection. I learned this when I attended a course at the foremost college on Wine Technology, at Geisenheim-am-Rhein, on 'The Nursing and the Development of Quality in Wine'. The knowledge gained there is embodied in this book. Winemaking is mainly an art and is easily learnt by anyone who takes trouble in his winemaking.

There is still much misapprehension as to what constitutes a good wine. Do we want a wine made from a mixture of fruits and vegetables, a veritable Christmas Pudding wine, or do we emulate the wines of commerce which are made from the juice of a single fruit—grapes, peaches, apricots, cherries or a variety of berries? Surely we can learn something from the commercial production of wine!

It may be of interest to point out that in California, where viti-culture is widespread, the commercial production and sale of fruit wines is, or was anyhow some years ago, greater than the

10

Preface

sale of wine made from grapes. This goes to show that wines from fruits other than grapes can be just as attractive as grape wines. Admittedly wines made from a single fruit may be in some way unbalanced; this happens also with wines made from grapes. By blending the finished wines, great improvement can be achieved. Skill in blending can only be learnt by experience which points to the desirability of studying wines so as to acquire a trained paláte. This can only be done by buying and drinking commercial wines and attending wine tastings provided so generously by the Wine Trade. I had the wonderful opportunity of attending one of the outstanding wine tastings given by Lebegues through an introduction by my friend Sir Guy Salisbury Jones. It was a unique experience to taste young red wines, many with a prevailing fruitiness, and some red wines almost reminiscent of black-currant wine. Such wines are not intended to be drunk young as maturing will bring about great changes with a loss of fruitiness and the development of red wine bouquet. I have experienced this myself during my early days of winemaking. A raspberry wine with a most delicious raspberry flavour and brilliant ruby colour became, after some years storage tawny in colour, and had lost all its fruitiness and developed a port wine flavour. The loss of colour was no doubt due to the absence of sulphite and the uptake of oxygen during maturing. Sulphite would have prevented this. In my early days I considered cleanliness was the only thing necessary to produce good wines but my attendance at the Geisenheim College taught me that no good wines, with the exception of sherry, are made without sulphite. Sulphite has an important role to play in wine quality and this is fully discussed in Chapter 6.

To produce wines of quality the choice of the yeast is important. Any yeast will ferment to a greater or lesser extent. All yeasts will confer their own bouquet on the wine and some yeast will be more effective than others in the clearing of a wine and thus incidentally make for ease in racking. Undoubtedly the flavour profile of the yeast chosen is all-important, and in 1948 I tested many different wine yeasts and at least five different Champagne yeasts. It was amazing how the latter varied in flavour. The final choice was a Haut Villier Champagne yeast as it conferred a delicate and fruity bouquet on champagnes, still wines and ciders. Even with a good and suitable wine yeast, a reliable recipe and a satisfactory

Preface

fermentation the wine can still prove unattractive. This is where the skill of the vintner is needed. It is not necessary to have a background knowledge of chemistry or biology to make good wines or nurse them to perfection; winemaking is first and foremost an art which can be learned by anyone. Admittedly a knowledge of science helps in understanding the processes of fermentation and maturing. In my earlier book, *Amateur Wine Making*, published by Faber and Faber in 1956, among other things the science of winemaking is discussed.

In this, a real beginner's book, a new approach has been made. Having over the last fifteen years dealt with beginners' problems and queries I have learned to understand their difficulties and the need for a gradual approach to the art of winemaking. In this book, theories and methods are discussed only after the practical approach has been made and the winemaker has been shown how to make four typical table wines. After this, matters which at first would appear puzzling become easy to understand.

As was not the case in the approach made in *Amateur Wine Making*, in *Better Wine Making for Beginners* tables and gravities are ignored except in the case of the sections on grape wine and champagne. Theory is discussed only after experience in winemaking has been gained, and much emphasis is laid on the nursing and care of wines and on blending. Although wines made by the recipes given here using the methods advocated should be free from faults, a short chapter on wine faults, their avoidance and cure, is included. For full measure the book also includes advice on the showing and judging of wines, home brewing, and the making of Aperitives and Liqueurs.

To make this book useful to American and to Continental winemakers, both metric and U.S.A. measures are given in addition to British measures. Of the 150 or so recipes, most have been used successfully by me with the exception of some using tropical fruit; these have been kindly supplied by winemaking friends in South Africa, Kenya and Rhodesia. I have also received recipes and valuable information from my dear friend 'Andy' Anderson, the founder and Director of Wine Art, Vancouver. I am indebted for much valuable advice to Professor Schanderl of Geisenheim, to Dr Beech of Long Ashton, to my husband for the reading and correction of the manuscript and to his encouragement and long-suffering patience in all my winemaking activities.

1

Wine—What is it?

The making of wine for home consumption is not a new craft. No doubt wines common in the olden days were similar to many of those made nowadays by amateurs. Elderberry wine is reputed to have been brewed in various university colleges in both Oxford and Cambridge where it was blended with Port wine, and no-one was any the wiser. Country inns brewed their own wines from indigenous fruit, and as a sign that wines were ready for sale a bush of gorse or whin was hung up outside the inn. Naturally when the wines were good the news soon got around and from this originates the saying—'A good wine needs no bush'. It is a known fact that in Portugal the growing of elderberries in winemaking districts is forbidden lest the Port wine producer be tempted to mix elderberries, which exhibit such intense red colour, with the red grapes having a less strong colour. It is also known that white wine made from rhubarb in the county of Norfolk, where much Champagne Rhubarb was grown, used to be exported to France for blending with the white wines in Champagne production. Fruit wines used to be sold in England until the Excise duty which was levied made this an uneconomic business; but gradually, because of renewed interest, fruit wines are again appearing on the market and are becoming appreciated on their own merits.

Wine, in the ordinary sense of the word, is a fermented beverage produced from the grape only. Otherwise the wine is given the prefix of the fruit from which it originates. Wines result from the interaction of yeast, which may be present on the fruit, and a sweet

13

liquid, such as the juice of the grape or of other fruits to which sugar has been added. The interaction which takes place and which is noticeable by more or less vigorous evolution of bubbles, is called fermentation. One can, therefore, say that wine is, in essence, a fermented grape juice. This is somewhat of an over-simplification because fermentation alone does not produce a wine fit for drinking. The fermentation has to be guarded or looked after or else the wine might easily turn to vinegar. Further-more, wines are not ready for drinking as soon as the fermentation is complete, but require quite a bit of nursing before they become wines fit for consumption.

Wine can be of different types such as light, non-sweet table wines—either red or white; sweet dessert wines—both red and white, such as Ports and Sauternes; Sherry-like wines and spark-ling Champagne type wines. The amateur can most certainly make wines of these various types and there are no inherent difficulties.

Wine, as mentioned, is produced by the action of a yeast on a fruit juice. If fruit is stewed with some sugar, after which any yeasts present on the fruit will have been killed, and is then left exposed to the air, after some days the juice will start to go cloudy and bubbles will be noticed. What in fact has happened is that yeasts which are floating about in the air, together of course with moulds and bacteria, have fallen into the juice and started the fermentation, that is, the conversion of the sugar into alcohol —this is the first step in wine production. This brew will, most probably, turn to vinegar as the usual precautions have not been taken, and furthermore, wild yeasts such as are found in the atmosphere are generally poor fermenters.

The first knowledge that the would-be winemaker must acquire, therefore, is of the nature of yeast and its function in winemaking. As early as 1858 the French chemist Pasteur studied the action of yeast on sugar and in subsequent years proved finally that yeast was the cause of fermentation, that is the conversion of sugar into alcohol. Without yeast there could be no fermentation. For instance, by boiling grape juice or any other sweet juice and storing it in a sterile bottle with a sterile closure, the juice could be kept indefinitely. If the bottle were allowed to stand open to the air then, after a while, bubbling would start, and this would be due to the wild yeast floating about in the air which had settled on the juice. On the other hand, if some yeast is added, then quite soon a

1 *Stages in clarifying. From right to left. Original fermentation, a deposit of yeast and impurities called 'lees'. Centre—deposit after first racking. Left—wine fined and brilliantly clear; deposit here consists of finings only*

2 *The Sanbri Hand Corker*

very vigorous fermentation will start, the sugar will disappear, and alcohol will be produced; this is the start of winemaking.

Frequently winemakers are advised to use baker's yeast but this may easily fail to produce a good wine. To ensure success a wine yeast, either liquid or grown on a jelly in a test tube, known as a tube culture, should be used. In fact, it is of the utmost importance only to use a reliable and guaranteed pure wine yeast. Many commercial yeasts are badly contaminated and dried yeast is normally not free from impurities.

There are available quite a range of wine yeasts and their particular suitability for specific wine types is discussed in Chapter 4, but for the beginner the All Purpose Wine Yeast is strongly advocated. The All Purpose yeast which I use is available both as a tube culture and as a liquid yeast, and must not be confused with many other All Purpose Yeasts now on the market. It has fantastic properties—it ferments at all temperatures, settles well to a sticky sediment which helps to clarify a wine, has the ability to produce high alcohol, and, last but not least, is a yeast with a wonderful flavour. It may astonish the beginner that yeasts have flavours, but anyone who has tasted some baker's yeast will know that this has a pretty strong taste and not an agreeable one. It is not the kind of flavour wanted in a wine, and it is bound to become fairly prominent at some stage of the winemaking process. Hence no-one wishing to make wines of quality will choose this yeast.

Let me state at once that simply the choice of a yeast such as a Sherry Yeast, Port Yeast or Champagne Yeast will not automatically produce a Sherry, Port or Champagne. The yeast will help by having a suitable flavour or other needed properties, but the fermentation must also be conducted in a suitable manner to produce a wine of the required type.

What else does a yeast do? First of all, the sugar—all or part of it, depending on the amount present—will be turned into alcohol. The more sugar present, the more alcohol will be formed; within reason that holds good, but too much sugar cannot be tolerated by the yeast. With, say, only 1 lb of sugar in the gallon of fruit juice, the fermentation will be lively; with 4 lb it will be a little less vigorous, and with 6 lb it may stop fermenting altogether. It is, therefore, in many cases advisable to start the fermentation with only part of the sugar and add the rest in several lots. This is called 'feeding' and is done when strong alcoholic wines are wanted but not in the production of Sauternes where the right amount of sugar must be added at the start of the fermentation.

When the yeast has converted all the sugar it can into alcohol, then it stops visible working, that is, fermentation ceases. There may be more sugar there than can be worked out, and in this case the wine will remain sweet. If all the sugar has gone, then the wine will be known as dry. It is not desirable for dry wines to have too high an alcohol content, so sugar additions for dry wines are kept deliberately lower than the maximum the yeast could ferment. The beginner will not need to know how much to add as the recipes will take care of that, ensuring that a suitable wine results.

As the yeast is of such great importance for the production of a quality wine, it is worth while taking trouble about it. When one considers how costly one failure in winemaking can prove, and as the major cost lies in the sugar and the fruit, the outlay on a wine yeast proves comparatively small.

2

Three Beginner's Wines: Orange, Apricot, and Apple Wine

As a preliminary canter let us make an ORANGE WINE. This is one of the easiest wines to make and oranges are available all the year round. The wine can also be drunk after two to three months. It should preferably be sweet and be made from the *juice* of the oranges only—whole sliced oranges produce a bitter wine and the oil in the skins often interferes with the fermentation. A really large juicy orange will contain about 4 oz of juice; then 10–12 oranges will give about 2 pints of juice. The juice is best extracted with a lemon squeezer and should be strained through a coarse nylon sieve or muslin. It is made up to nearly a gallon with water in which 3 lb of sugar have been dissolved. It is best to add about 1½ pints of boiling water to the sugar, stirring to dissolve, then adding another 2 pints of cold water. The volume will now be about 7 pints—this mixture should be put into a 1 gallon glass jar, as illustrated on page 20.

Next, one level tablespoonful of citric acid and one crushed Campden tablet should be added, followed by ½ teaspoonful of Yeast Nutrient, and a liquid All Purpose Wine Yeast. The juice should now be tasted and if not sufficiently sour some lemon juice or citric acid must be added. It should taste as sour as a fairly sharp apple. If it is lacking in acid at the start of fermentation, then the flavour of the wine will be poor. Then an airlock containing water in the bent lower tube must be inserted. This acts

Three Beginner's Wines: Orange, Apricot, Apple

Gallon jar used for fermenting

as a seal against the air, but allows the gas which comes off during fermentation to escape. Only the lower link of the airlock must be filled with water. If the airlock is too full, water can suck back into the fermenter.

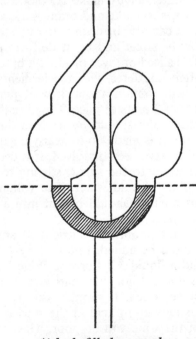

Airlock filled correctly

After a few days, the brew will go milky and may start to bubble. The jar can be given a slight shaking at intervals for the first two or three days as this will ensure that some more yeast will grow, and is as good as stirring. After this, the jar is left in a warm place, say an airing cupboard around 20° C., 68° F., for about a week. The milkiness which is first noted is due to a considerable growth of yeast. After a day or so gas will start to bubble through

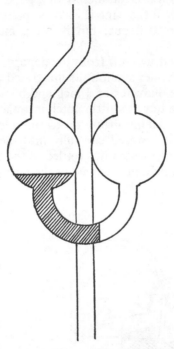

Airlock during fermentation

the water seal of the airlock. The container must not be disturbed now, as renewed shaking will delay the onset of the fermentation. After about a week of vigorous bubbling it is as well to move the jar into a cooler room for the fermentation to slow down. It must be left until the bubbling ceases—after this it should be tasted. If all the sugar has gone, another 1 lb of sugar is dissolved in $\frac{1}{2}$ pint of boiling water. This makes 1 pint of syrup. Half a pint of this syrup is added, and the wine is left again until bubbling ceases,

21

and then it is tasted. If it is on the sweet side the jar is filled up with about ½ pint of water and left at normal room temperature until the brew starts to clear through yeast settling out. If the brew is not sweet enough, then instead of water, the other ½ pint of syrup is added.

Now comes the hardest task which the winemaker has to face; that is, to resist the temptation to bottle the wine. It is not ripe for bottling, nor will it be stable. With a good All Purpose Yeast and a Yeast Nutrient the wine should be pretty clear when most of the yeast has settled out: but if not it must be left until it clears.

The wine is now drawn off from the deposit. This is done quite easily by using a rubber syphon, as illustrated below. The rubber tube should have a diameter of ⅜ inch and be no less than 1½ yds. long. It is desirable to put a little notch into the end of the rubber tube to prevent it sucking firmly on to the side of the gallon jar. The notched end is lowered carefully into the jar to about one inch above the sludge which has settled at the bottom.

This tube is best held in the neck of the jar by a clothes peg. By

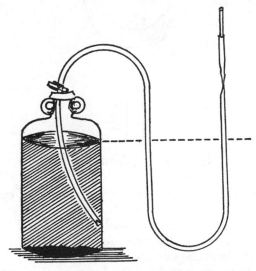

Use of Syphon—narrowing indicates where to pinch the rubber tube

Three Beginner's Wines: Orange, Apricot, Apple

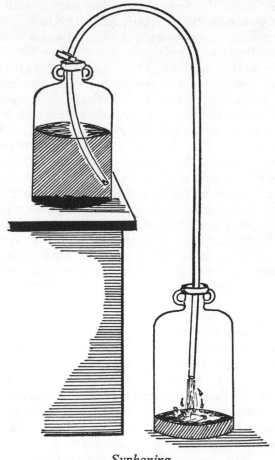

Syphoning

holding the tube in a loop and just below the level of the wine, a
slight suck will ensure that the loop gets filled with wine. Pinch
firmly where indicated. By now lowering the tube into a jug or
pail or a clean fresh gallon jar, nearly all the liquid can be syphoned
off.

Provided the syphon is long enough its management is quite easy.
When the open end of the syphon is lifted above the level of the
liquid in the gallon jar, the liquid will cease to flow, and when
lowered below the level it will start to flow again.

Three Beginner's Wines: Orange, Apricot, Apple

Racking. After the fermentation has ceased and the yeast settled the wine may still be slightly hazy. This haze is due to proteins (albuminous matter present in all fruit) which have not been entirely absorbed by the initial yeast growth in the juice. By now removing the yeast, called *racking* the wine, and giving the wine some air, new yeast will grow and absorb these haze-forming proteins, thus making the wine clearer. To help the yeast to grow, aeration is desirable, so at the first racking no Campden tablets should be used; the wine should be splashed into the receiver, which will remove any gas still in the wine. Therefore the rubber tube should not be lowered far into the receiving vessel which should preferably be a clean gallon jar. Finally the jar should be filled to the top with water, to make up for the loss in volume due to the sediment, and left with its fermentation lock sealed by fresh water for a couple of months when a new yeast deposit will be noted. If there is any sugar left in the wine this is liable to lead to further fermentation and it is therefore important to rack the wine again after two to three months. If the container is in a warm place, two months' rest suffices; if in a cold place, racking after three months is advocated. Even dry wines will contain traces of fermentable sugar, in either free or bound form.

It may be found that the orange wine is clear after the fermentation has ceased. Nevertheless it should, after racking, receive a further two months' period of storage.

At the second and further rackings the wine should be treated with half to one Campden tablet,* prior to syphoning off quietly into a fresh container which must be topped up with water if some of the wine, or of a similar sweet wine, is not available.

As a sedimentary sticky yeast has been used for this orange wine it will have formed at the second racking a firm deposit which will make it possible to rack practically all the wine off by gently tilting the jar. The last dregs are preferably drawn off into a small jug and after a day or so the supernatant liquid can be poured off into the storage jar.

A dry wine can be bottled after the second racking. A sweet wine needs one or two additional rackings. Prior to bottling a crushed Reductone tablet should be added to the gallon of wine.

It is as well, however, to test the wine for stability by putting a

* Some winemakers prefer to keep the sulphite content of their wines down to a minimum.

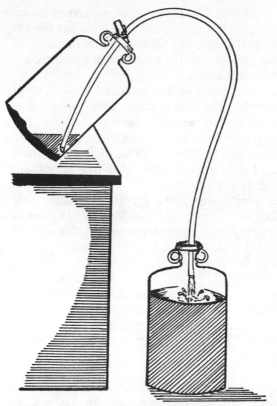

Emptying jar by careful tilting

couple of ounces into a small bottle, corking and leaving it in a warm airing cupboard for a few days. If no pressure develops then the wine is ready for bottling; but first draw a little off into a cup and crush into this a Reductone tablet. Return to the jar and leave for twenty-four hours. After this the wine can be syphoned straight off into bottles. Orange wine hardly ever needs fining to improve its clarity.

Bottles should have been well washed and as soon as filled should be corked with new corks which are preferably inserted by a proper corker—see page 67 and Plate 2. Then the corks can be tied or wired down and the bottles must be stored lying down. It is as well to inspect the bottles after three months.

Three Beginner's Wines: Orange, Apricot, Apple

A sweet wine which has only been racked twice may develop a haze or deposit; this proves that the wine has been bottled a little too soon. In this case the wine must be returned to a gallon jar for another period—say for a further two or three weeks maturing and then bottled again.

To recapitulate. Squeeze out sufficient oranges to give two pints of juice, strain, add sugar, citric acid, Campden tablets, Yeast Nutrient and a wine yeast. Ferment in the warm for a week then remove to cooler conditions. Leave to clear, rack into clean containers, leave two or three months, rack again, and add a Campden tablet. Leave preferably another two months, add a Reductone tablet, and bottle.

Orange wine made in the foregoing manner will *not* have an orange flavour, but will be more like a semi-sweet or sweet table wine. The orange flavour comes from the skins and it is quite easy to produce an orange-flavoured wine by soaking some thinly pared orange peel, not the white part, in the wine until sufficient flavour has been extracted. This is most conveniently done by tying the peel into a square of butter-muslin and suspending this in the wine.

Nothing has yet been said about the role of Yeast Nutrient, Campden tablets or Reductone tablets, but this will be left for discussion in Chapter 6 under the heading 'Wine Making Ingredients'.

Having now made a simple wine, let us progress to something a little more complex: not more difficult, but needing a bit more attention. The second hurdle is an APRICOT WINE. Apricots will make a really attractive dinner wine but the amount of fruit used should be kept low. Fresh apricots should be peeled and the stones removed. Peeling is facilitated by pouring boiling water over the fruit. Two pounds are sufficient for one gallon. If dried apricots are used then ½ lb suffices.

Apricots, like all stone fruit, peaches, plums and damsons, contain a considerable amount of pectin. Now pectin is needed for jam making but it is not needed and is actually undesirable in wine making. A pectinous juice is thick and therefore the yeast cannot act properly, and the fermentation may be very slow. As it progresses the pectin will settle out in a thick cloud and will spoil the wine. It is quite easy to get rid of the pectin, even in a finished wine, by the addition of a pectic enzyme, but it is always preferable to use a pectic enzyme right at the start when making wine from fruits rich in pectin.

Now to practical details for the production of *Apricot Table Wine*. To give a well-balanced apricot wine several additions are needed. First of all Pectozyme to break down the pectin, then citric acid to confer desirable acidity on the juice, Campden tablets to give good wine flavours, Grape Tannin to confer an agreeable astringency to the wine and, of course, the fruit, water, sugar and the wine yeast. Yeast Nutrient is required when fermenting the fresh fruit, and a vitamin yeast food is needed to ensure an energetic fermentation when using dried or tinned fruit.

Detailed directions for making an Apricot Wine from dried apricots.

Half a pound of dried apricots are brought to the boil with 2 pints of water and simmered until completely soft, emptied into a plastic pail, and 2 pints of cold water are added. Next, about 1 tablespoonful of Pectozyme and ½ lb sugar are stirred in, followed by ½ teaspoonful of Yeast Energizer. The mixture is allowed to cool to blood heat then a crushed Campden tablet and a liquid wine yeast are added. The container is now covered by a lid, or by some butter-muslin tied over it, and left in a warm place such as an airing cupboard for four days, stirring twice daily. This is called 'pulp fermentation'. The broken-down pulp is next strained through a coarse linen or hessian bag which can be pressed and the residue discarded. The liquid, which has been collected in a gallon jar, is next mixed with 2 lb of sugar dissolved in 2 pints of warm water, then there is added a dessertspoonful of citric acid and half a level teaspoonful of grape tannin, and the whole made up to a gallon with water. There will be sufficient yeast present as it will have passed through the pores of the hessian bag. The jar is now kept at room temperature and fermentation will continue at first vigorously and then a little more slowly, and cease in a few weeks' time. The gallon jar should have been provided with an airlock with a water seal and the cessation of fermentation will be noted by the lack of bubbles round the circumference of the liquid or passing through the water seal of the airlock.

Now the wine, which will still be far from clear owing to the yeast remaining in suspension, must be put in a cool place—this will help the yeast to settle and the wine to become clearer. When

Three Beginner's Wines: Orange, Apricot, Apple

it and all the debris from the fruit has settled, the wine is syphoned off from these lees—as the residue is called—into a clean gallon jar. If necessary, some water is added to fill the jar to the top, an airlock is inserted and the wine is left for another two months. After this time it should be much clearer and a second yeast deposit should have formed—if not the wine must be left for another month. It is as well to add half to one crushed Campden tablet prior to syphoning the wine off the deposit. Generally the wine should now be clear enough to bottle, but unless it is really brilliantly clear, suitable finings should be used to clarify it completely. The best finings to use are Serena Wine Finings which consist of two solutions 'A' and 'B' to be added to the wine. Serena Finings are referred to later, see Chapter 8. The finings interact to form a milky solution which, as it settles, will pull all the hazes down with it and give a wine which is star bright. Such a wine will be more mature, more rounded in flavour and considerably more stable than an unfined wine. A Reductone table can now be added to the clear wine which is drawn off from the deposit into a clean container through a rubber syphon. After a day or two the wine is ready for bottling.

Prior to bottling the knowledgeable winemaker will taste the wine—it may be lacking in acid, or the very fact that it is entirely free from sugar may make it a little too dry for some tastes. Allowing for the fact that wine on storage will improve and develop definite wine flavours, nevertheless a wine which is too dry is not necessarily to everyone's palate. This problem can be overcome in two ways—either the wine can be sweetened with glycerine or a special Dry Wine Improver, or the dry wine can be blended with a sweet wine. Glycerine is a natural constituent of all wines to a greater or lesser extent and ½ oz of glycerine added to each pint of wine will give a slightly sweeter and smoother wine with more body. Special Dry Wine Improver also gives a certain amount of body to the wine. If the wine is not sweet enough, then the only remedy is to blend it with a sweet wine which has fermented out—store it for another month to see that there is no re-fermentation, and then bottle. When blending sweet and dry wines which are stable, there is always the chance that fermentation will re-start after blending. The use of a stabilizer can prevent this but the addition of Campden tablets is no guarantee at all that there will not be renewed fermentation. If instead of blending with a sweeter wine, sugar is added, then the wine must *not* be bottled as there is *bound* to be renewed fermentation. The reason for this is that in dry wines, where the alcohol content is kept deliberately low, the yeast has not reached the alcohol level which it normally produces in sweet wines. As soon as more fermentable sugar is introduced by addition or blending, new yeast can grow and start to ferment.

Another method of dealing with this impasse is to sweeten the wine by sugar or by blending with a sweeter wine only a few days prior to consumption.

From the foregoing recipe it will be noted that a pectic enzyme such as Pectozyme was required. Whenever there is a high proportion of pectin present, as in all stone fruits, and also in quite a few berry fruits, such as gooseberries and currants, a pectic enzyme helps extraction and the fermentation. It is sometimes also used when making wine from grapes as it helps in giving a better colour extraction and greater yield of juice. The skins, which are pectinous, will break down with the addition of a pectic enzyme and more of the juice and tannins will be leached out.

It will also be noted that instead of Yeast Nutrient, as in Orange wine, a Yeast Energizer is added. This Energizer is a yeast food which is rich in vitamins and is needed for all fruits in which the vitamins have been destroyed by drying, concentrating, canning or boiling or for fruits which are naturally low in vitamins like Bilberries.

To Recapitulate. An Apricot Wine is produced by fermenting on the pulp with the aid of a pectic enzyme, adding citric acid, vitamin yeast food, Campden tablet, grape tannin and wine yeast. Fermentation is carried out for four days on the pulp in the warm, then the mixture is strained and allowed to ferment on. The wine is racked two or three times with the usual addition of Campden and Reductone tablets. If too dry it is blended with a sweeter wine or sweetened prior to consumption.

Now let us consider stepping up production by making 5 gallons of APPLE WINE. Many beginners start their winemaking in 1 gallon quantities—this is an advantage, as normally 1 glass gallon jars will be used which allow the winemaker to see what is happening. This is not quite so easy in barrels. On the other hand, it is just as quick to make 5 gallons and instead of having six bottles of wine, thirty would result. Also it is more convenient to draw the wine off from a barrel through a tap than to have to use a syphon. In addition, wines in larger containers have less tendency to spoilage through air, while a wooden barrel helps the wine to mature.

The wine is made in a 4½ gallon cask, also known as a pin, and is made from any kind of cooking or eating apple, but about a quarter of the apple content should be in the form of crab apples— the ornamental Crab is quite useful. Failing that half a teaspoonful of grape tannin per gallon should be added to the juice. Thirty to forty pounds of apples are thoroughly washed and minced by passing the fruit through a coarse mincer or fruit pulper; the resulting pulp is transferred to a polythene bucket which should contain 10 Campden tablets* dissolved in a little water. This must be stirred into the pulp when each lot comes from the mincer. A wine yeast must next be added and should be preferably in the form of a starter (see Chapter 4). After a few hours the pulp is strained through a coarse hessian bag and pressed in the fruit press. The pulp is loosened, a couple of pints of water are added, and the pulp is again pressed. No fresh yeast need be added as the yeast is able to pass through the pores of the bag. The juice should be made up to 3 gallons with water if necessary. Next, two tablespoons of citric acid and one of Yeast Nutrient are added, and if the apples used did not include crab apples, one level dessert spoon of grape tannin should be added. Sugar is added in two lots and it is a convenience if this is kept available as a ready prepared syrup. Six pints of syrup are produced from 6 lb of sugar and 3 pints of warm water. Six pints of syrup are stirred into the above and when this has fermented out can be followed by another 6 pints. This will nearly fill the 4½ gallon cask but the second fermentation will not produce much foam so the cask can with advantage be nearly full to the top. An airlock should of course be fitted at the beginning of the fermentation.

This wine, after the fermentation has finished, may be sweet enough, but it rather depends on the original sugar content of the apples used. If not, then some of the wine is drawn off into a winchester or ½ gallon jar lightly plugged with cotton wool or fitted with an airlock, and some more strong syrup is added to the cask. It is suggested that 4 pints are drawn off and replaced by another

* Apples yield a better wine if 2 Campden tablets are added to the pulp required for each gallon.

Three Beginner's Wines: Orange, Apricot, Apple

4 pints of strong syrup (made from 4 lb of sugar and 2 pints of water).

In every case the syrup added must be well mixed in by stirring. To the 4 pints of wine drawn off add 8½ oz of sugar dissolved in some of the wine so as to bring it to the same sugar content as the wine in the cask. It is useful to have over more wine than needed to fill the barrel as, with the usual racking procedures, there are bound to be losses; and a barrel containing sweet wine should preferably be filled up with wine of the same strength and sugar content rather than with water.

The wine is left to clear and when practically clear can be taken off the yeast deposit by drawing off through the tap. This wine will be mixed with the wine from the ½ gallon container and a crushed Campden tablet is stirred into it. The barrel is washed out and refilled with the wine, which should then be tasted. It may be lacking in acid or lacking in tannin—which can then be added. It is left in a cool place for two to three months, again racked off from the yeast deposit, and 4 Reductone tablets are added to the whole bulk which is returned to the container. As this is a sweet wine it is just as well to leave it a further two months and if necessary fine it (see page 64), and then bottle a few days after fining.

To Recapitulate. Apple Wine is made from the juice of apples only. The fruit is minced and pressed, the juice mixed with sugar, citric acid, Campden tablet, Yeast Nutrient, tannin if crab apples have not been used, and a wine yeast. Five gallons are produced to fill a 4½ gallon cask, known as a pin, which leaves some wine over for filling up. The usual racking is carried out as with the previous two wines, and the wine is bottled.

3

Grape—The Wine of Wines

(*The Hydrometer and other Equipment*)

Having now shown you how to make a wine from orange juice, a wine from a pectinous fruit which has been fermented on the pulp for four days, and an apple wine produced in a 4½ gallon wooden cask, let us briefly consider winemaking from grapes.

Wines made from grapes grown in this country or from imported Cyprus grapes or even greenhouse grapes, generally contain too little sugar to give a dry wine of suitable alcoholic strength. Although we aim in this book to give recipes which do not require the use of the hydrometer, when making wine from grapes it is very desirable to employ one. Other fruits used for winemaking mostly contain relatively little sugar, and frequently too much acid, so that water has to be added. The effect of diluting the quantity of sugar present in the fruit when compared with the amount of added sugar makes its presence insignificant; on the other hand, when using mainly grape juice, which can vary in gravity from 45 to (in extreme cases) 190 degrees, only by using the hydrometer can one be sure of making a wine of the right type and alcohol content. Although in general 1 lb of sugar to the gallon of grape juice is needed when making wine from English-grown grapes, sometimes the sugar content of the grape is higher, and less sugar will be needed. Good dry white and red wines can be made from juices the gravities of which range from 75–90 degrees; or, expressed as specific gravities, the reading on the hydrometer will be 1·075 to 1·090. Dry wine made from a juice

3   *Hydrometer and jar*

4   *Components of a Swiss press*

5 *Wine Making Equipment*

where the reading is 1·100 will be rather alcoholic, and dry wines are more attractive if they contain less alcohol. A juice with a gravity of 75–90 is preferable for a dry wine.

To enable the required sugar addition to be made without referring to tables the winemaker need only remember that the addition of 5 oz of sugar to the gallon of juice will increase the gravity by 10 degrees. Therefore if the gravity of the juice is 45 then to bring it up to 75 it requires the addition of 3×5 oz of sugar, or near enough 1 lb. The volume of the juice will be increased from 1 gallon to 1 gallon 10 oz as each 1 lb of sugar in solution occupies a volume of half a pint or 10 oz. The extra amount will be useful for topping up.

Not everyone will have outdoor grapes available but it is possible to buy fairly cheaply grapes which have gone slightly mouldy in wholesale fruit markets at the end of the week. It will mean picking out the mouldy fruit and using 3 Campden tablets to each gallon of juice. A word of warning, though: do not buy mouldy red grapes, as mouldiness there can lead to bitterness. Imported dessert grapes generally are somewhat lacking in acid, which can be added as tartaric or citric acid. The small imported Cyprus grapes are wine grapes of a suitable acidity, while grapes grown outdoors in this country very often have a juice a little high in acid. If this is so, a small dilution with water, say about 2 pints to a gallon of juice, will bring the acid down to reasonable proportion. Obviously the gravity of this juice will have to be taken after dilution with water.

Let us say you have about 10 lb of grapes available. The berries are pulled off the stem and crushed by hand or by pounding with a pestle or a wooden potato masher. The pulp is put into a coarse hessian bag and pressed, preferably in a fruit press. As soon as the juice is drawn off two or more Campden tablets are added to each gallon of juice. For mouldy grapes three to four tablets are advocated. It is not easy to say the amount of juice 10 lb of grapes will yield; it depends on the grapes and the efficiency of the press. To ensure that the juice still retained by the pulp is fully extracted. the pulp is loosened and mixed with a pint of water and repressed. To test the gravity of the juice a little is strained through a nylon sieve and transferred to a hydrometer jar when a hydrometer is inserted gently into the liquid; where the spindle emerges the number is read. This will give the gravity of the juice which is next

33

adjusted to a gravity of 80 or 90 by the addition of sugar. Then the grape juice which has been treated with two crushed Campden tablets is left in a cool place overnight for most of the debris to settle out. The juice is then decanted from the debris, an All Purpose wine yeast and half a spoonful of Yeast Nutrient are added, and the juice is divided between a gallon and a half-gallon jar. Airlocks should be inserted and the jars then brought into a warm place, about 20° to 24° C., 68 to 75° F., when the juice will start to ferment. Partly clarifying the juice as above slows down the fermentation a little, and a better wine results. If this clarification has not been carried out then the fermentation temperature must be kept much lower to slow down the fermentation. As soon as the foaming becomes less the larger container is filled up from the small one and the surplus kept in a bottle plugged with cotton wool. When fermentation ceases the wine is brought into a cool place and left there for a week or two to clear, after which it must be racked. All grape wines must be refrigerated to bring down tartrate crystals. No other fruit juice contains this compound known as Cream of Tartar. This must be thrown out, and it can only be done by keeping the wine for a few days at freezing temperatures. Next the wine is racked off these crystals and treated with another Campden tablet, left two to three months, racked again and tested for stability. Unless it is brilliantly clear it must be fined prior to bottling. This is how a dry white table wine is made, and it can be made from the juice of either white or red grapes. It is also possible to make an attractive wine from the prunings of greenhouse grapes although these contain no sugar. A recipe for this is given in the recipe section (page 22).

To produce a red wine the fermentation must be carried out in the presence of the skins of sound red grapes. The fruit is pulped and the pulp is treated with two Campden tablets. Next the gravity must be ascertained by pressing some of the pulp through a piece of coarse linen and testing the juice with a hydrometer. The required amount of sugar is then added and ½ teaspoon of Yeast Nutrient. The pulp is next transferred to a polythene bucket and allowed to ferment there until the colour is rich red, but not until all the sugar has gone. This fermentation must be done in a cool place. The pulp should be pushed under several times a day and the container must be kept well covered. The pulp will always rise to the top and be liable to develop vinegar if it is allowed to collect as a thick mass, called a cap, which floats on the juice.

The cap will contain a low percentage of alcohol, which, if exposed to the air, is quickly turned into vinegar. It can be kept submerged by a perforated board which fits the container and allows the juice to percolate up through it and down again over the cap; and by these means vinegar formation will be prevented. Another method is to tie the pulp loosely in some butter-muslin, weight this with a stone tied inside the muslin, and see that the whole remains below the surface of the liquid. Extraction of the

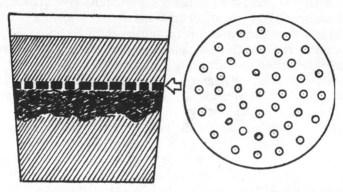

This illustrates a sinker, i.e. a perforated board which holds the pulp below the surface of the liquid. It should be heavy enough not to float up. If not it must be weighted with a stone

colour in this case has to be helped by squeezing the muslin bag occasionally.

Red wine made from indigenous grapes tends to be over-acid and unbalanced in flavour. In other words the wine will lack tannin. This can be either added as tannin or be introduced by fermenting some elderberries with the grapes in the proportion of 1 part of elderberries to 2 parts of grapes. The acidity is best over-come by adding from 1 to 2 pints of water to each gallon of the extracted grape juice, i.e. to each 14–15 lb of grapes.

It is of course possible to make sweet wines from grapes but details of this will be given when discussing wine types.

Grape—The Wine of Wines

In the foregoing we have introduced you to winemaking by easy stages, and now the winemaker will not find it difficult to understand the advice given on procedure, adjustments of juice, choice of yeasts, addition of pectic enzymes, Yeast Energizer or Nutrient, Campden tablets, citric acid, Reductone tablets and Serena Wine Finings. In later chapters we will explain the value and great importance of racking, the advantages of blending, and the possibilites of stabilizing and maturing the wine.

It is not necessary to spend a lot of money on winemaking. Although we have mentioned previously a number of useful winemaking ingredients, most of these, once acquired, keep indefinitely and are needed only in small amounts. It is of course a great help to have a wine press and a fruit pulper, and for those who make much wine their usefulness cannot be over-rated. Of the two the latter will be more useful as it will grate up all hard fruit much more quickly and effectively than a mincer, and will break up grapes and berry fruits if you use a suitable second roller designed for crushing rather than grating.

The fruit pulper illustrated here is quick and effective. The metal-studded roller is used for apples and pears while the fluted roller is intended for grapes and is suitable also for gooseberries. Failing this, a household mincer can be used for pears and apples while berries can be crushed by a potato masher. The pulp is then put into a bag and transferred to the press where the juice is extracted by pressure. This must only be applied gradually as a liquid cannot be compressed. After the initial pressure juice will exude and further pressure can then be applied. To repeat, it is not possible to obtain the juice from grapes or berries until these have been squashed or broken. On no account must the pulp be put into the press without filling into a bag, as the pulp will be forced through the staves so that the juice will contain too much debris. It is also important not to apply too much pressure at the start of pressing; it can be increased when some of the juice has run out.

It is, of course, possible to break up berry fruits by hand, or by treading, or by the use of a pestle or wooden potato masher or a stout wooden club. If the grapes are trodden, clean rubber boots are a help and if the treading is carried out in the bath, be sure not to pull the plug from force of habit until the pulp and juice have been scooped out!

Hard fruits such as pears and apples are minced, but on no

36

account must their juice, or that of grapes, be boiled. Stone fruits should be freed from their stones and can be softened by boiling water, while good extraction is ensured by the addition of a pectic enzyme.

From this it will be seen that it is possible to prepare fruits without much equipment. Fruits like elderberries, which do not contain much pectin, can be brought to the boil and it is perfectly safe to use aluminium vessels for boiling but not for fermenting. Apart from aluminium or stainless steel, no other kind of metallic vessel must be used. Both copper and galvanized iron can spoil a wine but, fortunately, the winemaker is now able to use polythene pails, buckets, jugs and funnels—none of these will affect the wine in the early stages. I would on no account advise storing the wine in polythene containers, or fermenting wine in polythene beyond the first stages when the alcohol content is low, as not all polythene is free from plasticiser with an undesirable flavour.

The minimum requirements, to my way of thinking, are a 5 gallon polythene bucket, a 2 gallon one, a 1 gallon jug and a 2 pint jug; all these are, nowadays, almost household equipment. A plastic bowl, several polythene funnels and a colander are also a help. Coarse hessian bags measuring 14″ wide by 18″ deep, which can be draped over the rim of a 2 gallon bucket or over a colander, are useful. The other items essential to winemaking are a few 1 gallon jars and 4½ gallon or larger casks, several airlocks and a rubber syphon. (See Plate 5 facing page 33.)

In addition the winemaker will require proper wine bottles which hold about 26 oz, so that 1 gallon will fill six bottles; also corks. It is possible to secure flanged corks as illustrated: and they can be inserted without a corker; but for wines other than Sherries a properly inserted straight-sided cork, requiring a proper corker, is a greater protection for the wine. Plastic corks are favoured by some winemakers but frequently are a poor fit and will cause spoilage of the wine.

The foregoing equipment is all that is needed, with the exception of a corkscrew, which is really the most important item to satisfy the soul of a winemaker.

4

Wine Yeasts and their Functions

First of all let us consider the nature of yeast and its origin. The two photographs facing page 33 illustrate the shape and size of a true wine yeast and a baker's yeast. An actively growing yeast pushes out little protuberances called 'buds', which, when grown to full size will frequently separate from the mother cell, but sometimes may remain attached and thus form chains. Most yeasts will bud from several points of the cell, starting at the pointed end, but sherry yeast tends to polar or di-polar budding; budding can only be observed under the high power of a microscope.

Yeasts have several stages of development. They can be in a state of rest, and as such are found in the soil and on fruit or foliage. Or they may be actively growing, which they do in a nourishing liquid like a fruit juice when they are in the presence of air. On the other hand, they can use the sugar present in the fruit juice and convert it into alcohol and carbon dioxide gas which bubbles off. The latter process, which is called fermentation, only takes place when the air in the juice has first been used up for yeast growth.

When yeast acts on a sweet fruit juice, yeast growth will soon become apparent due to the liquid, which previously had been fairly clear, gradually becoming milky. This can often be noticed when leaving fruit juices exposed to the air. Wild yeasts, together with mould spores and bacteria, float about in the atmosphere and will settle on the juice, where they will first start to grow and subsequently bring about fermentation. When this takes place bubbles will be noticed gradually rising to the surface. Unfortunately, however, this fermenting liquid will almost certainly go to vinegar because vinegar bacteria will have got into the juice at the same time as the yeast. These bacteria will convert the alcohol formed by the yeast into vinegar.

To allow fruit juices to ferment in a haphazard manner is not the way to produce a sound wine. To get rewarding results a reliable and genuine wine yeast free from contaminants should be used. Another source of vinegar bacteria are the small fruit flies which settle on any sugary liquid; they are carriers of vinegar bacteria and so must always be excluded.

A further precaution which must be taken is to exclude all air during fermentation. This is extremely important, as air is needed for the conversion of alcohol into vinegar. Fermentation vessels supplied with air locks are safe, and as a further precaution a Campden tablet added at the start will prevent air from affecting the wine.

It is always wise to start the fermentation with despatch, and this can only be done if the yeast is added in an actively fermenting condition and in sufficient quantity. The most lively yeasts are those grown on agar slopes, followed closely by good quality liquid yeasts. Dried yeasts are sometimes very slow in starting, or even quite inactive. Any active yeast added directly to a fruit juice, without activating it in a starter bottle, will start a fermentation after a shorter or longer period. It is obvious that, particularly in the case of fruit juices which have not been sterilized, wild yeasts must be present. These will take up·what nourishment is in the juice and will start the fermentation unless an actively fermenting wine yeast has been added. In such a case the wine yeast will dominate the fermentation. If juices have been sterilized by heat or Campden tablets the wine yeast can be added direct to the juice. Nevertheless, the onset of fermentation is delayed when only a small amount of a wine yeast is added to the juice, and the importance of getting an adequate amount of wine yeast into the prepared juice as soon as possible cannot be over estimated. This can only be done by preparing a starter bottle beforehand and adding the contents of this to the juice as soon as the juice is ready.

Preparation of a Starter. To prepare the starter all that is needed is to transfer the yeast to some sweetened orange juice (1 tablespoonful of sugar to 4 to 6 oz juice) sterilized by boiling, transferred to a 10-oz bottle while hot, plugged with cotton wool and allowed to cool. The yeast is then added; it can be either a liquid yeast or an agar slope which is transferred to the juice. Alternatively the yeast on an agar plug can be dispersed in some water by three quarter filling the test tube with some boiled and cooled water, replacing the rubber bung, and shaking vigorously. The yeast will be removed by the water which is then added to the starter bottle. The bottle is left in a warm place without shaking for a few days, when it will be fermenting well, and then most of it is emptied into the ready-prepared juice. The bottle can be replenished with some more boiled and *cooled* sweetened orange juice and be ready for further use after a week. If not wanted it can then be stored in the refrigerator and activated a day or so before use by adding a teaspoonful of sugar dissolved in water and leaving it in a warm place. Orange *squash* must not be used for a starter as it is preserved to prevent yeast growth. Canned orange or grapefruit juice may be used.

Bakers' Yeast. Until it was realized that a culture can be made to last, thus reducing the cost of wine yeast considerably, many winemakers, as already mentioned, used baker's yeast either in paste form or as dried yeast. Although baker's yeast will start to ferment quickly, it will never confer vinous quality. Furthermore, it is powder yeast, that is to say, light in weight, and will tend to float up at racking time and make a wine cloudy and difficult to rack.

Wine Yeast. The reader may wish to know how these wine yeasts originate. They come, of course, from wine-growing districts, but for use elsewhere they have to be propagated from these special areas and kept as pure culture strains. The yeasts mentioned by name in this book refer to those which have been specially cultured as above and sold by the Grey Owl Laboratories. They have all been specially selected. from a wide variety available, for their ability to produce wines with the specific characteristics associated with their name, with good flavours and with high alcohol content.

Writers on amateur winemaking have mentioned that sherry yeast is a poor fermenter, but this is not the case with Grey Owl sherry yeast which is capable of producing high alcohol levels as well as a good sherry flavour.

All Purpose Wine Yeast. This yeast tends to clarify a wine even during the fermentation and it settles to a firm and sticky deposit, making for ease in racking. It is available both as a liquid yeast and as an agar slant, and is suitable for most wines. The name All Purpose Yeast was coined for it by the Grey Owl Laboratories and although this title has now been generally adopted, there is no guarantee that all yeasts with the same name are the same yeast. Nor is the All Purpose Yeast, as has been stated, a mixture of yeasts but is a pure strain. Mixed yeasts are useless as they cannot be relied upon to remain present in the same proportion.

Port Yeast. Some yeasts have the property of taking up the pigments of a red wine and making it tawny—this is not desirable for table wines but the ability to produce tawniness is a very marked characteristic of a true Port yeast which should always be used for sweet wines intended to be Port-like in character. Port wine is of course a sweet rich and alcoholic red wine, but the use of the correct yeast alone will not produce a wine resembling Port. It is not possible to make a true Port wine from grapes grown in this country as they are too low in sugar and tannin and too high in acidity. Also it is not economically feasible for the amateur to make a true port as this is done by stopping the fermentation by the addition of alcohol. Nevertheless something very like a Port can be produced from elderberries—see Elderberry Port recipe, page 100. Also Port type wine, page 116.

Malaga and Madeira Yeast. Tawny wines, but with slightly different flavour, can also be obtained by the use of Malaga and Madeira yeasts. These yeasts, together with Port and Tokay, belong to the class of yeasts known as powder yeasts. They are less sedimentary than the All Purpose, Burgundy, Pommard or Sauterne yeasts and also tend to autolyse more easily. This means they impart their own characteristic flavour to the wine.

Pommard Yeast and Burgundy Yeast. While discussing red wines, consider the dry red wines, the Clarets and the Burgundies. For these one must on no account use a Port yeast. In wines like these there is every advantage in retaining as much colour as possible, and the more sedimentary a yeast is, the deeper will the colour be. Pommard, Burgundy and All Purpose yeast are the only ones suitable for red table wine. Pommard will no doubt produce a wine with most colour, while the other two will produce more bouquet.

Sauterne Yeast and Tokay Yeast. These two yeasts are particularly suitable for sweet wine although the Tokay yeast is markedly strong in flavour and not suitable for dry wines; the flavour is far too strong and it should only be used for really sweet white wines. The Sauterne yeast is suitable for all dry and semi-sweet wines; it has a fine flavour but is not sufficiently strong to become predominant.

Chablis Yeast. This is a wine yeast of particularly good flavour with a tendency to produce a certain amount of acid, and has proved a help in producing wines from honey, from green gooseberries or from flowers, making the wine rather more attractive than do other yeasts. Such a yeast is particularly suitable for Red Rose Petal Wine, which even without the addition of fruits, and with only a small amount of lemon juice, produces a superb wine.

Champagne Yeast. To make a wine with sparkle does *not* require a Champagne yeast—any yeast will render a wine sparkling. If it is not intended to remove the yeast from the bottom of the bottle, then a sedimentary yeast is by far the best to use. As this is a sticky yeast, if the wine is chilled and care is exercised before and during serving, the bulk of the wine can be poured off clear, leaving the yeast behind. Sparkling wines like Champagne are wines which have undergone a second fermentation in the bottle. In commercial practice the yeast is removed from the wine by a special method called 'disgorging'. Care is, of course, taken that the sparkle is retained in the wine, and Champagne production is a skilled process. However, despite its inherent difficulties sparkling wines freed from the yeast deposit are being produced successfully by amateurs. This will be discussed under Champagne in Chapter 12. If it is intended to disgorge, then a Champagne yeast *must* be used, as this yeast is sandy in nature and heavy. It will not stick to the bottom, nor will it tend to float up and cloud the wine as a powder yeast would, but it can be shaken into the neck of the bottle to settle to a compact mass which can be removed by appropriate means. During the process of Champagne production much of the yeast decomposes; thus the flavour of Champagne is strongly influenced by the yeast. Champagne yeasts can vary very much in flavour, as has been proved by the author who tested eleven different Champagne yeasts before finding one which gave the desired flavour.

Pectin Removal through Yeast. Many yeasts can deal with small amounts of pectin. If they could not do so, no fruit wine would clear. Even wines high in pectin will sometimes clear after several rackings but there are some yeasts which can cause the precipitation of a pectin clot. I myself came across the phenomenon in a Liebfraumilch yeast which was tested in an apple juice and produced a thick precipitate of pectin. This does not mean to say that other yeasts bearing that name will behave in a similar manner, but it does show the need for assessing the performance of wine yeasts before supplying them to winemakers.

Starch removal through yeast. Many recipes which contain cereals or starchy fruits like bananas, direct that the ingredients be boiled with water. This gelantinises the starch and such wines are difficult to clear. Only malt extract will convert this starch to sugar but the flavour of malt is hardly desired in a wine. Starch hazes can be avoided by using a special yeast called Saccharomyces Oryza which actually attacks the starch. This yeast is now obtainable as Cereal Wine yeast and should prove most useful for cereal wines.

Sherry Yeast. It is possible to make a wine with sherry character from any wine yeast, provided that the wine is sufficiently oxidized during and after fermentation. On the other hand yeasts do vary in the amount of aldehyde they produce and it is the ability to achieve a high level of acetaldehyde, a normal constituent of sherry, that is the characteristic of a good sherry yeast. This yeast also produces high levels of alcohol and is able to yield dry and sweet wines with an alcohol content ranging from 18 to 21 per cent. Some sherry yeasts do, under certain conditions, develop a thick wrinkled skin on the surface of the wine, known as a 'sherry flor'. Special flor yeasts are now available, but just as in commercial sherry production the development of a flor film cannot be guaranteed even with a flor yeast, even so is its occurrence in amateur sherry production equally problematical. Note that the sherry flor film is never thin and white, nor does it creep up the sides of the container. Such a film which breaks easily is commonly known as 'flowers of wine' and is caused through mycodermi. Wine with a mycodermi film soon develops a vinegar taint and becomes completely spoilt.

In the foregoing, enough had been said to show that the choice of yeast is important. This is not only because of the flavour that the yeast can impart, but also because of its ability to help in the production of certain wine types, to facilitate and enhance clarification, and to produce desired levels of alcohol.

43

5

Fermentation and other Yeast Activities

Having now experienced several fermentations and witnessed the growth of yeast during the process of winemaking, the winemaker will be able to understand and apprecia.e the process of fermentation.

First Stage: a clear fruit juice growing milky due to intense yeast growth.

Second Stage: the juice is in a ferment through the evolution of bubbles of gas known as carbon dioxide gas.

Third Stage: a heavy deposit of yeast and other debris is noted, leaving the juice clearer than it was.

Fourth Stage: the first violent fermentation is slowing down, and on tasting the 'must' or 'brew' it will be found to be almost free from sugar, or anyhow much less sweet.

Fifth Stages: the fermentation ceases and after a while the wine becomes much clearer. (This has already been discussed under 'Orange Wine').

After this it is usual to take wine off the yeast, that is rack the wine. Inspection of the racked wine after a month or two will show that it has become still clearer, and a fresh deposit of yeast has formed. Some of the yeast food still left in the wine will have been taken up by the yeast, and through this the wine will have become more stable. It will now contain no more, or anyhow much less, food for further yeast growth. Such is the case provided that—*and this cannot be stressed strongly enough*—the wine is racked off the yeast deposit not later than three months after the previous racking. If the wine is left on the yeast longer than this, the yeast will decompose. This is called 'autolysis', and when it happens the proteins of the yeast will dissolve in the wine and render it unstable (as fresh yeast will feed on these proteins and may eventually start a renewed fermentation).

Racking stabilizes a wine and it should be done at two to three monthly intervals. Too frequent racking does not give the yeast time to impart its characteristic flavour to the wine. If a young wine is racked immediately after the fermentation ceases a new yeast deposit will form in twenty-four hours. As an experiment such racking was repeated with a Blackberry wine each day: a deposit formed daily but got progressively less, and after the fifth racking no further yeast would grow in the wine; in fact the wine, although sweet and not very high in alcohol, was completely stable. Nevertheless it was not at all wine-like in quality but tasted more like blackberry juice with a somewhat inky flavour to which some sugar and alcohol had been added; nor did it become at all clear. The same Blackberry wine racked at three-monthly intervals became brilliantly clear and was just as stable after three rackings. In fact it was a lovely wine. This shows that proper racking procedure has an influence on wine quality, and that yeasts do a lot of good to the wine even after they have finished fermenting. They clean a wine and clarify it, produce small quantities of glycerin and acids such as succinic acid, and confer some of their flavour and their vitamin B content on the wine. Furthermore, wines which have developed slight 'off' flavours, due perhaps to exposure to air, can be vastly improved, or, to use the correct term, 'freshened up', by stirring some clean and recent yeast deposit into the stale wine. After a few days the yeast will have settled and the wine can be racked in the usual manner.

Anyhow, enough has been said to show that suitable yeasts are fundamental to good wine production and the flavour of the yeast is bound to add something to a wine which has undergone repeated racking at the right intervals. As has been mentioned earlier, yeasts also attack the colouring matter in a wine, especially the powder yeasts like Port and Malaga. Other yeasts have the ability not only to ferment but also, after the fermentation is completed, to rise to the surface and to form a film which gives sherry character to any wine, whatever fruit it is made from. The study of yeast is a fascinating one, and most rewarding.

Yeast and Fermentation Temperatures. Although some yeasts ferment equally well at lower temperatures, on the whole the rate of fermentation is accelerated by increase in temperature. This is in large measure due to the fact that the warmer the must is the

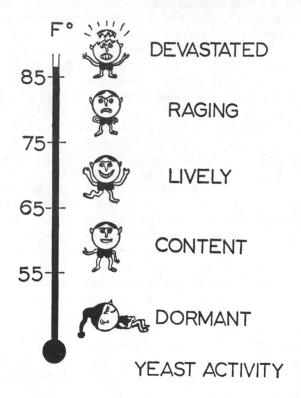

more rapidly the gas, which has an inhibiting effect on the yeast, will disengage and the livelier will the fermentation become. That yeast activity is affected by temperatures is most fortunate. The winemaker, by fermenting at different temperatures, has a great measure of control over his wine. Too fast a fermentation, that is when the gravity drops more than 20 degrees a day, can be slowed down by bringing the fermenter into a cooler place. Too slow a fermentation, that is a gravity drop of less than 5 degrees a day, can and should be speeded up by fermenting in warmer surroundings. The fermentation temperature has an effect on the flavour of a wine. Cool fermentation, that is round about 15° C., 59° F., will produce fruity wines. Higher temperatures tend to give vinous flavours, but over 28° C., 82° F., the yeast will tend to die, although there are some yeasts which stand up to these higher temperatures. The artist's drawing records yeast behaviour in an original manner. (By courtesy of Mr J. H. Toule, the Founder of the Oakfield Wine Society, Bristol).

On the other hand, the fermentation of the yeast can be slowed down even in the warm by not letting the gas escape, that is by fermenting under pressure. This is sometimes done in commercial wine production, and if the pressure builds up yeast will actually cease to ferment until some of the gas is allowed to escape.

Yeast Growth and Alcohol Production. Another characteristic of yeast, which is not generally known, is that yeast will not ferment if the oxygen content of the juice is too high. Sometimes the amateur winemaker is nervous and thinks that his juice is not going to ferment. He shakes the container and, hey presto, the carbon dioxide gas which is accumulating in the juice or the starter bottle is removed by shaking out, air is taken up, and the fermentation is slowed down or stopped. The aeration will cause fresh yeast to grow and it may take a week or two before the juice will start to ferment again. Only by leaving the container undisturbed until the yeast has got the juice into the deoxygenated state which is favourable to fermentation will the process continue. It is possible to arrest incipient fermentation for weeks on end by frequent agitation, so that more and more yeast is grown. In fact a grape juice to which a wine yeast starter was added was allowed to ferment normally and took fourteen days to complete its fermentation, this resulting in a good wine. The same juice with the same wine yeast which was shaken every day for a fortnight had grown so much yeast in that time that it fermented to dryness in two days. It was absolutely undrinkable. So—leave your fermenting vessel undisturbed for good results. On the other hand if the fermentation is sluggish, stirring and aeration will improve yeast growth and the subsequent fermentation will be more satisfactory.

Sometimes, when adding repeated quantities of sugar to the wine, it may so happen that the fermenter is too full. The wine will then have to be drawn off into a larger container prior to mixing with some more sugar or syrup. This will again inhibit fermentation through the air absorbed during transfer, and it will take a week or so before fermentation re-ensues; but it is nothing to worry about. However, in general it is better to use a fermenter of a size large enough to take repeated additions of syrup, as this interferes less with the subsequent fermentation.

Yeast and Alcohol Producing Capacity. Quite a few fantastic claims have been made for the alcohol-producing capacity of a wine yeast. The truth is of course that a good wine yeast can produce as much as 21 per cent of alcohol by volume in special circumstances. These are when the must is high in fruit content with added nutrient and when the sugar is added in stages. On the other hand, where the food content of the juice is low, the identical yeast will not produce more than 13.5 to 15.5 per cent of alcohol. I have done this with an elderberry juice. By adding all the sugar at once I obtained a sweet wine with 15 per cent of alcohol, just right for a dessert wine. The same juice by feeding produced a wine with 21 per cent alcohol, which is Port strength. It is all a question of the conditions being right for optimum yeast growth. Where food or aeration is low, then yeast growth may in some cases be insufficient to ferment out a juice even if the sugar content is low. This is called 'sticking' and can also be brought about by premature racking, that is, by racking while the fermentation is still under way. Similarly, when there is no sugar there can be no fermentation. Also fermentation even under the best conditions of yeast growth must stop when the alcohol is as high as the yeast can stand. Yeasts vary in their alcohol tolerance. Sedimentary yeasts are more alcohol tolerant, while powder yeasts are far less so. The winemaker is given this information to help him to interpret any abnormal happenings, but he need not be worried if these chapters on yeast behaviour prove a little difficult to understand. All the recipes appearing in the later portion of this book are intended for the beginner, and so adjusted that the desired wine type will be achieved.

Many of the recipes will appear comparatively lower in fruit content than those published in other wine books or journals. The compiler has never had much time for 'Christmas Pudding' or 'Kitchen Sink' wines. There are two schools of thought on this; (1) put in all you can think of and get a wine with high alcohol content and a kick, but which will have no perfume or bouquet;

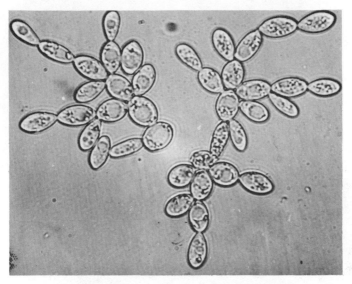

6　*Wine Yeast magnified about 700 times*

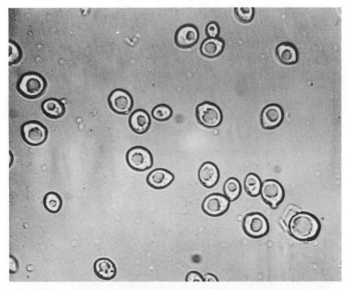

7　*Bakers' Yeast magnified about 700 times*

8   *Fruit Pulper; the studded roller is used for hard fruit, the fluted for soft fruit*

and (2) keep the fruit level down and force the yeast to work in starving condition and obtain a wine with perfume and vinosity, and, what is more important, of the right alcohol content. The desirable alcohol content for different wines will be discussed in Chapter 11, 'Wine Types'.

The winemaker can try this himself by making an Apricot or Peach Wine with 1 lb and with 3 lb of the fresh or canned fruit to the gallon. The one with the lesser fruit content will be more attractive and probably less alcoholic, while the higher fruit content may yield a wine with too much alcohol. It does sometimes happen that even commercial wines have a higher alcohol content than desirable. In this case the Frenchman will add water to his wine before drinking as he knows this will improve it. Many a time has the author been able to demonstrate at competitions that wines which are too alcoholic become vastly improved in flavour on the addition of a little cold water. After all grape juice is not particularly rich or heavy but it produces a satisfactory wine of suitable alcohol content. Consequently if wheat or bananas were added to the grape juice the result would not be a light, Hock-like table wine but something resembling jungle juice. So beware of overloading your must with too much fruit. Exceptions are when sweet wines like Ports are wanted. If it is intended to make Port from elderberries, for instance 6 lb of fruit to the gallon is not too much but half this quantity would suffice for a table wine.

Sticking Fermentation. Many amateurs get very worried when the fermentation suddenly ceases. This is often a normal occurrence which rights itself after a month. If gravity determinations had not been made, these temporary stickings would never have been noted. Stickings which are practically permanent are those where the wine has been racked while still fermenting (sometimes done commercially to retain sweetness in a wine and produce sticking), or it can be due to the addition of too much sugar at the start of winemaking. This is easily overcome by diluting a gallon of wine with 1 or 2 pints of water. Sticking can also be due to overheating and thus killing the yeast. The latter defect cannot right itself and the fermentation must be promptly restarted by making a fresh starter and adding small quantities of the wine, say half a pint at a time, to the starter until the fermentation is vigorous, and continuing in this fashion until all the wine is fermenting well. During sticking the yeast attacks the colouring matter of a wine and this

Fermentation and other Yeast Activities

is particularly undesirable in dry red table wines. In wines where the yeast has been killed by heat, sticking will often occur when the alcohol is still low, with consequent danger of vinegar formation. It is obvious, therefore, that on the whole sticking is undesirable; but if the wine is protected from air, fermentation will frequently start up again after a period of temporary sticking, and the wine will, if anything, be much improved in flavour. Examples with recorded hydrometer readings in *Amateur Wine Making* (Faber and Faber) show the occurrence of sticking.

Yeast and Sugar content. Earlier on we have mentioned that the sugar content of grape juice may range from gravities of 45 to near 190. At lower gravities of up to 100 the yeast will ferment quite normally, but when gravities exceed 140 to 150 the fermentation can become exceedingly slow or cease altogether. Yeast which has been exposed to high sugar content becomes weakened and does not ferment too well, thus wines made from grape juice with a high initial gravity will take some years to complete their fermentation. They undergo repeated periods of sticking followed by yeast autolysis, new yeast growth and renewed fermentation. Such is the case with the Noble Wines and the Trockenbeere Auslese Wines of commerce (see *Amateur Wine Making*).

6

Wine Making Ingredients

Fruit Acids. Although it is possible to make a wine just from fruit juice, sugar and a yeast, there is no guarantee that such a wine will be attractive. It may have 'off' flavours; this is frequently the case when the juice has lacked acid and will quite likely result in a wine with a medicinal tang. It is therefore important to add some acid juice, such as that of lemons, or else add citric acid. Another acid which can be used is tartaric acid. This is somewhat harsher in flavour, but some prefer it. On the other hand it has the disadvantage that in the presence of potassium salts it may lead in the cold to a crystalline deposit which is a nuisance.

It is highly undesirable to add malic acid, as this is easily broken down to give a wine with a flat taste. Citric acid has many advantages in winemaking, not the least of which is that any traces of metallic contamination in a wine are prevented from making the wine hazy. The choice lies therefore between citric acid and tartaric acid, and contrary to some published information, neither acid helps yeast growth. How much to add depends on the acidity of the fruit or other ingredients used, but for wine made from vegetables or cereals $\frac{1}{2}$ to $\frac{3}{4}$ of an ounce to the gallon is required.

Yeast Nutrient. This is one of the winemaking adjuncts which should never be omitted when adjusting the must, but in some instances the Nutrient must be replaced by a vitamin yeast food or Yeast Energizer. Winemakers may wonder why yeast needs a nutrient. The simple fact is that there is plenty of nourishment

51

for the yeast in many fruit juices but the yeast cannot break down the albuminous matter present in the juice without the help of ammonium salts. A nutrient of a suitable formula should only contain ammonium salts. Nothing else is needed or desirable and the addition of potassium salts and tartaric acid or tartrate must be avoided, as otherwise the wine has to be chilled to remove acid potassium tartrate (cream of tartar).

Yeast Energizer. Wine yeasts require a certain content of vitamins for their own growth and for sound fermentation. Fruits which have not been boiled, dried, concentrated or canned, mostly contain sufficient vitamins for adequate fermentation. Where vitamins are lacking, as in canned or dried fruits or low as in bilberries or where much dilution has occurred, then the addition of Yeast Energizer is called for. Where fermentations are too sluggish or cease prematurely (so-called 'sticking') Yeast Energizer is particularly valuable.

The effect of adding a vitamin yeast food where fermentations stick is not always noted immediately. It may take about fourteen days before the full effect takes place, as the yeast has first to absorb the vitamins. After this the increase in activity can be enormous; this was noted in the case of fermenting an unripe honey which had already fermented in the jars. When used for winemaking it simply would not ferment, but where energizer was added a most satisfactory fermentation ensued, but only after fourteen days.

Grape Tannin. This is an important constituent in winemaking. It is naturally present in the skin of grapes and other fruits. When fermentation takes place in the presence of the skins, a considerable amount of tannin will be extracted. Such wines will be robust, that is, will not tend to spoil, and they will have more body than a wine lacking in tannin. Furthermore, the flavour will be preferable to that of a wine with hardly any tannin content. Most fruits contain some tannin, but frequently insufficient. In that case, grape tannin should be added. It is best to add most of this prior to the fermentation, as subsequent addition may render a wine hazy. Where tannin has been used prior to or during fermentation, subsequent addition of tannin should not affect the clarity of the wine. Only small amounts are needed, and $\frac{1}{4}$ to $\frac{1}{2}$ teaspoonful to the gallon is generally adequate. The only criterion as to the amount to be added is arrived at by tasting.

Wine-making Ingredients

Pectic Enzymes, such as Pectozyme. These can vary somewhat in their activity, and the winemaker is advised to stick to a well-known brand and to follow reliable directions. Pectic enzymes break down the glutinous matter present in fruit in a matter of hours at the right temperature (40° to 60° C.), and in general they are completely effective after reacting with the fruit juice for a few days in the airing cupboard or a hot cupboard. These enzymes will also clarify a wine which is thick and cloudy due to the presence of pectin. To ascertain whether the wine is suffering from a pectin haze a test can be carried out by adding double the quantity of methylated spirits to a small quantity of the wine. The presence of pectin is proved if a deposit settles out after twenty minutes or so, or if the wine goes milky. Throw away the small amount of wine so tested.

Campden Tablets. There are some winemakers who talk with scorn of the use of Campden tablets in winemaking. They speak slightingly of chemicals in wine, quite ignoring the fact that the active principle in Campden tablets has been used for centuries in all commercial wine production. The burning of sulphur in casks produces a gas which is present in known amounts as a salt in Campden tablets. It has been proved by commercial wine producers throughout the world that wine made in the absence of sulphite has considerably less flavour acceptance than where there has been an addition of sulphite. Normally speaking, two to three Campden tablets added to a gallon suffice, one at the start of fermentation and half to one added at the second and third rackings. Fruits which brown easily need more sulphite and if fruit is mouldy, and particularly where grapes are used which have become mouldy, the quantity of Campden tablets to be used should be at least doubled at the start. Although these have a certain sterilizing or preserving value, their chief function is to stop the wine from taking up air and thus developing 'off' flavours.

Note: Strong solutions of sulphite—say 20 Campden tablets in a pint—are used to sterilize mouldy casks or other vessels, but such strong solutions are never added to a wine.

Reductone Tablets. These are a fairly recent addition to the range of ingredients important in winemaking. They contain ascorbic acid (vitamin C). They are, like Campden tablets, an antioxidant—that is, they prevent the wine from taking up air. Some fruits, such as apples, pears and strawberries, in fact all fruits containing

53

enzymes causing browning, tend to take up more air than other fruits and require a double dose of Reductone tablets to prevent the wine from oxidizing and getting sherry-like.

Serena Wine Finings. To fine or not to fine, that is the question. Wines which are slightly hazy, mainly because they are rather young or because they were taken off too soon from the yeast, need to be clarified. There are many ways of clearing a wine. Some commercial winemakers use Isinglass—this requires great skill in handling and great experience in knowing when it can be used with success. It is consequently not recommended to amateurs. Others carry out a two-stage fining, employing grape tannin and gelatine. No definite amounts can be laid down, so about a dozen tests have to be put on before finding the optimum amounts to be added to any particular wine. This is hardly a feasible method when wine is made in small amounts. Still another method is to use Bentonite or Kieselgur. In this case a mechanical filter press is a necessity. Filtration and clarification with asbestos pulp expose a wine to air over a long period and may spoil it. The method is gradually being abandoned for fining. The most successful finings for amateurs are those where known amounts of two liquids such as Serena Wine Finings are added to the wine one after the other. As the precipitate which is formed settles down it entrains any hazes that are present and thus clarifies the wine. Such finings are successful in every case where the wine is finished but not clear, provided that the haziness is not due to pectin, although they can remove slight amounts of pectin, but they are bound to fail where this is excessive. If a pectic enzyme is added subsequently to fining the wine will go brilliant through the combined activity of the finings and enzyme. These finings not only render a slightly hazy wine brilliant, they also mature and round off a wine, making it at the same time less harsh and more stable.

Serena Wine Stabilizer. Here the question is, which wines need stabilizing? Theoretically speaking, no wines should be bottled until they are stable, but both domestic and commercial wines can and do sometimes become unstable after bottling. This may be either due to air uptake during bottling or to the wine not having been racked over a sufficiently long period to ensure stability.

Commercial wine producers go to great lengths to stabilize their wines and to bottle under near sterile conditions. The amateur could stabilize his wine by pasteurizing, but this frequently produces hazes and 'off' flavours. Pasteurizing is carried out by heating the wine in the bottle up to 140° F., taking 20 minutes from cold to this temperature, then holding at that temperature for 20 minutes, and taking 20 minutes to cool the bottle down to room temperature again. This is, of course, quite an undertaking without proper facilities. The difficulty can be overcome by the addition of a stabilizer which is of vegetable origin and entirely wholesome to use.

Wine Flavourings. The above adjuncts are frankly all the competent winemaker needs. Wines should be attractive through the proper choice of fruits, yeast and fermentation procedure. On the whole, artificial flavours or spices are not needed in winemaking, though sometimes a mature wine can be improved by judicious blending with wines of different character. On some few occasions flavours can also confer some special quality on a wine. Flavours such as orange, sherry and port are useful. The last-named flavour can also be used to improve red wine.

7

What to Ferment and How

Flowers. Fruits. Vegetables. Cereals.

It is possible to make really good wine from almost anything provided that the juice is properly adjusted. Whether it is extracted or prepared from fruits, flowers, vegetables or cereals, or even from walnut, rose or tea leaves, by adding the required amounts of acid, a vitamin yeast food, and where needed tannin and fermenting with a suitable yeast, all such wines can be attractive.

Flowers. Flowers and leaves, unlike fruit, contain little natural yeast food and it can be an advantage to add this; perhaps in the form of 1 lb of sultanas to the gallon, or in the form of grape, apple, orange or other fruit juices.

Many winemakers have a preference for flower wines as they have found them to clear well; this is mainly because there is no pectin present in the flowers, and if fruit is added the content of this is kept low enough for the yeast to deal with the pectin. The amount of flowers used will vary according to the taste of the winemaker and may range from 1 to 4 pints of flowerheads or florets to the gallon. Elderflowers have a particularly penetrating odour and taste and their discreet use, say one pint to the gallon, avoiding the green stems of the florets, gives sufficient bouquet to the wine. Flowers are particularly easy to handle and the range in this country is wide; easy-to-follow recipes are given in Chapter 12.

Fruits. Fruits are generally the best ingredients from which to

56

make a wine and may be fresh, dry or canned. The preparation of the fruit varies according to its nature. Some fruits yield a good juice after either crushing or mincing. Soft fruits such as grapes and other berry fruits are crushed, and hard fruits like apples and pears are minced prior to pressing out the juice. Other fruits need softening with boiling water or bringing to the boil with water. Elderberries can be boiled without any harm. Stone fruits like plums, peaches and apricots are rich in pectin and therefore need pulp fermentation with the addition of Pectozyme. Dry fruits such as dates and figs have to be disintegrated with warm water but raisins and sultanas should be minced prior to treatment with hot water. Citrus fruits should only have their juice extracted; the use of the whole fruit is not desirable as the resulting wine will otherwise be far too bitter, while the oil present in the skin may lead to fermentation difficulties. Rhubarb is classed with fruits and I have developed a new method of extracting the juice with dry sugar which produces a wine of suitable acidity, free from pectin and oxalic acid and with a fine flavour. The table on page 58 shows the appropriate treatment for various fruits, though no hard and fast rules can be laid down.

Vegetables. The range of vegetables available is again very large, from peapods and parsley to parsnips, carrots and beetroots. The last-named vegetable tends to earthy flavours but this can be lessened by boiling the beetroots until soft in an open vessel, removing the skins and tops and crushing to a pulp. A few days of pulp fermentation will give sufficient colour to the wine. Beetroots are made preferably into a sweet wine, and any earthy flavour will disappear on maturing. Carrots and parsnips are peeled, boiled and when soft are pulped and strained. The juice only is fermented, sometimes with added orange or lemon juice, some sultanas or raisins and the usual addition of acid, tannin and Campden tablets. If the vegetables have only been boiled until they are just soft the amount of pectin present is low enough for the yeast to deal with it. If the boiling has been excessive and the juice is thick, then a pectic enzyme is needed at the start of the fermentation.

Parsley by itself is too low in food value to support good yeast growth, and for winemaking the juice of oranges and lemons must be added to the cooled brew prepared by boiling the parsley and straining it off. This addition helps the fermentation, and if

What to Ferment and How

TABLE I

JUICE FERMENTATION

Wash fruit, mince and press out juice, but don't use boiling water or boil

Apples
Pears

Crush, add a Campden tablet, press out juice

Grapes
Raspberries
Ripe Gooseberries
White Currants

Pour boiling water over the fruit to just cover. Then mash and press

Elderberries
Bilberries
Green Gooseberries
Raspberries
Mulberries
Elderberries and Bilberries may be boiled and strained

Soften by boiling water and press or draw juice by covering with dry sugar

Rhubarb

PULP FERMENTATION

Crush clean fruit, add Campden tablets and ferment on the pulp until sufficient colour is extracted

Red Grapes
Cherries
Redcurrants
Blackcurrants
Blackberries
Sloes
Strawberries

Pour boiling water over the fruit, when luke warm add some pectic enzyme, $\frac{1}{4}$–$\frac{1}{2}$ lb sugar, Yeast Energizer and a wine yeast. Ferment on pulp from 1–5 days

Apricots, fresh or canned.
Peaches, fresh or canned.
Plums, fresh or canned.
Pineapple, fresh or canned.
Damsons (1 day only)

Soak in hot water. Leave 24 hours prior to pulp fermentation.

Dry Figs
Dry Dates
Bananas

Mince and soften with warm water, prior to pulp fermentation

Sultanas
Raisins
Other dried fruit

58

sufficient sugar is added and an All Purpose wine yeast is used, the wine can be surprisingly like a Sauterne.

Cereals. Personally I can see little sense in making wine from cereals. Apart from sweet corn which has enough sugar to warrant turning it into wine, cereals like rice, barley, wheat and dried maize really only act as a protein food for the yeast, and either dried fruit or fruit juices together with sugar are required to turn the cereals into wine. One can of course use malt extract to convert the starch into sugar just as is done in beer making, but this has to be done at the right temperature, and is hardly worth the trouble. A special Cereal Wine Yeast of good flavour is a help in fermenting cereal wines and will prevent starch hazes (see page 43).

Many wine enthusiasts use cereals and even potatoes to help give body to the wine, but the winemaker is advised to restrict his winemaking to one or not more than two ingredients, be they fruit or vegetable juices, and learn what to expect as a finished product. It is then possible to achieve desirable results by blending. Mixtures of fruits with cereals and vegetables must at the best produce variable results.

There is a strong case for using mixtures of fruits when they balance each other. High tannin fruits mixed with acid but less tannin-containing fruits and fermented together often give surprisingly good results.

8

Racking, Stabilization, Clarification and Fining

Racking and Stabilizing. Although the technique of racking has been outlined in the making of orange wine (page 24) it is of such fundamental importance that it is discussed here again. In many recipes winemakers are instructed to bottle their wines as soon as the fermentation finishes. Invariably these bottles will blow their corks or if the corks have been tied down then the bottles are likely to burst. Wines when they have finished fermenting are neither stable nor attractive. When the yeast has converted as much sugar as it can to alcohol, all yeasts, whatever their nature, will start to settle and the wine will start to clear from the top. A powder yeast settles slowly while a sedimentary yeast may settle even while the fermentation is under way. When there is no evidence of a ring of bubbles round the circumference of the liquid, and it is known that the fermentation has gone on without interruption, that is without sticking, then one may safely assume fermentation to be complete. As soon as the wine clears from the top it may take a week or so for the yeast to settle, after which the wine should be drawn off the deposit, or in other words, racked. This racking is one of the most important factors in producing wine quality, and is of course necessary to make a wine stable. Repeated racking and judicious use of sulphite (Campden tablets) and ascorbic acid or vitamin C (Reductone tablets) are of paramount importance in developing vinosity and in maturing a wine.

60

Racking, Stabilization, Clarification and Fining

What happens after racking? At the first racking, which should be done without adding a Campden tablet and by splashing the wine into a clean container, the somewhat cloudy or slightly hazy wine is drawn off from the debris of decomposed fruit or vegetable matter. In other words the wine is cleaned up. It is put into a fresh container and filled up to the top with spare wine, or if only little filling up is to be done, with water. Having splashed out all the carbon dioxide gas and encouraged some aeration, some more yeast will grow and this new yeast will feed on the haze still present and thus the wine will become much clearer. The wine is racked again after two months but a half to one Campden tablet* is added to each gallon prior to racking. This time the wine is *drawn off quietly without splashing*. If the wine is dry and star bright and does not deposit any yeast within a month, then it can be bottled.

One Campden or Reductone tablet should be crushed and added to each gallon prior to bottling. If it is not brilliantly clear the wine is best fined prior to bottling. Even if a wine is quite stable and bright, to leave it in bulk for another two months prior to bottling will generally produce a great improvement. So much for dry wines.

It is not possible to ensure stability in sweet wines or for that matter improvement in quality by only two rackings. If the wine is kept in a cool place, racking at four three-monthly intervals is sufficient, but at room temperature the racking should be carried out at two-monthly intervals. Here again the first racking should be with aeration followed by the addition of half to one Campden tablet prior to the second and third rackings and a Reductone tablet prior to bottling. Sometimes a wine is not stable after three rackings, and only testing will show if there is danger from re-fermentation through a fresh yeast deposit. This, as mentioned earlier, is done by putting a little of the wine in a small bottle in a warm airing cupboard. If no deposit forms in a week the wine can be bottled. At each and every racking the fresh container must be filled bung full with some wine of the same kind hence the desirability of making a little more wine than a gallon or 4½ gallon to start with. Normally wines are completely stable after sufficient racking provided that the wines are made with a

* I always use the larger amount of Campden tablets, but many winemakers prefer the lesser.

61

minimum of fruit and discreet use of nutrient. Wines rich in food substances tend to go on fermenting and to stabilize them is not always easy. In old-fashioned recipes this was no problem as brandy was added to the fermented beverage, and this prevented re-fermentation. This method of stabilization is to be shunned both on account of cost and of the undesirability of such a high alcohol content in wines.

Pasteurization. When it is not possible to get a wine entirely stable by racking, nor in extreme cases by the addition of a stabilizer, then the only method to follow is pasteurization in bottle. This is done in commerce, but wines must first be tested for heat stability. If they produce a precipitate or haziness when heating an ounce or two to 140° F. the wine must be fined and then tested again before filling into bottles. Pasteurization is carried out as follows. The bottles of wine without corks, are stood in cold water in a boiler with a false bottom. The water must reach up to the neck of the bottles. The water is brought up to 140° F. taking 20 minutes to reach this temperature, kept at this for 20 minutes, and then brought down to room temperature during the next 20 minutes. Corks which have been sterilized in approximated 1 per cent Sulphite solution, i.e 12 tablets to 10 oz water, are inserted loosely prior to cooling the wine and driven home when the wine is taken out of the water. Such wines should be quite stable.

Occasionally wines which are apparently quite stable, develop a little gas in the bottle some time after bottling. This may be due to what is called a malolactic fermentation which some wines undergo, but in general this only happens when juices have been too rich or too much laden with cereals and other nutrients. Some ferments which cause the wine to go 'petillant' like this can cause a small amount of fermentation in bottle although no yeast deposit has formed. Such wines, although stable, are not suitable for entering into competitions as a judge is bound to fear that they may be unstable and blow their corks.

Clarification. Hazes can be due to protein matter, pectin, starch or metallic contamination. Proteins are present in all fruits and the scum which separates out in jam making is due to this white of egg or albuminous protein. During fermentation and after racking yeasts can absorb these haze-producing proteins but not all wines can be cleared by repeated racking: persistent hazes have to be

Racking, Stabilization, Clarification and Fining

treated by specific means. The most common cause of haziness is pectin. If fruits are used which are rich in pectin, as are all stone fruits, then it must be removed. If the fruit is sound and is mashed in the cold, sulphited with a few Campden tablets and a good sedimentary wine yeast is added during pulp fermentation, the juice will become thinner and most of the pectin will break down. This is because fruits themselves contain a pectin-splitting enzyme. Cold preparation is somewhat risky as fruit can have undetected blemishes where vinegar bacteria may be lodging, as for instance vinegar-sour plums, and it is safer at least to pour boiling water over the fruit and then use an enzyme at the start of fermentation. Even then some winemakers are unsuccessful in removing the pectin, chiefly because they use the enzyme under too cold conditions. The pectin destroying enzymes can be added to the must at a temperature of 50° C. but this is too high a temperature for yeast addition. Both yeast and enzyme can be added to a must at 30° C. and keeping the fermenter in a warm plaee for three to four days ensures that all the pectin is decomposed. If a finished wine shows a pectin haze then it must be treated with one tablespoonful of Pectozyme and left in a warm place for four days. After that the wine must be fined.

Other hazes can be due to starch when a similar treatment with Amylozyme can overcome the trouble. Here the cure can produce off-flavours and it is better to use a yeast which attacks starch during the fermentation. Metallic hazes should never occur as it can only be due to the use of unsuitable utensils. Citric acid will clear metal hazes but cannot remove a metallic taste. Treatment of the wine with 2 to 3 oz of bran to the gallon sometimes effects improvement. The bran has to be strained off and a flannel jelly bag is often the quickest way to do this.

Other methods of clarifying a wine, such as mixing with filter aid like Kieselgur, Supercel or Bentonite, necessitate subsequent filtration. This, when done domestically on a large volume of wine, exposes the wine to far too much air and should be avoided. Treating the wine with asbestos pulp is a sounder method as it can be quite quick. About ½ oz of asbestos pulp is mixed with cold water and drained off through a funnel lightly plugged with cotton wool. The funnel is filled up with more water and the drainings are tasted to see that they are free from asbestos taste. Then some wine is poured into the funnel and allowed to drain. This wine will be diluted by the water retained by the pulp. It should therefore not be bottled. By now filling the funnel up with wine and keeping it filled the rest of the wine will come through quite quickly and be ready for bottling.

Fining. Although commercially Isinglass is sometimes used it is not always successful and cannot be recommended to amateur winemakers. Since the development of Serena Finings I have quite given up any other finings and hardly ever use asbestos pulp. A wine can be normally rendered brilliant with one treatment of these finings provided there are no gross amounts of pectin or starch present, but if after two days the wine is not brilliant it is syphoned off from the deposit of finings and given a second treatment. So as not to lose any of the wine the small residue is first put into a conical measure when after a day or so some more clear wine can be poured off and the very last dregs can be filtered through a No. 5 filter paper. This is a slow but very fine filter and its action can be speeded up by superimposing a No. 1 filter paper on the inside of the filter and filtering through both. The No. 1 filter catches the coarser particles and prevents the No. 5 filter from becoming clogged up. Just as asbestos pulp requires washing, so filter paper is not fit for use until it has been thoroughly washed.

When the wine appears clear it should be inspected with a Bendalux lamp in a dull light or taken into the dark and inspected by transmitted candlelight. By either of these methods the slightest haze will show up.

Sometimes wines, after chilling, throw down crystals of cream of tartar, also called potassium hydrogen tartrate. This salt is present in all grape wines and can be present in wines prepared with a nutrient containing tartaric acid and a potassium salt. It is wise therefore to chill all grape wines before bottling.

To recapitulate. Lack of clarity can be due to protein hazes which should be cleared by yeasts during the racking procedure, or if still present are removed by Serena Finings. Pectin or starch hazes are due to faulty technique which can be cured by treating with the appropriate enzymes, while metal hazes should not occur when using wood, glass, porcelain or plastic vessels and containers. Crystals of tartrate can only be removed by chilling and decanting.

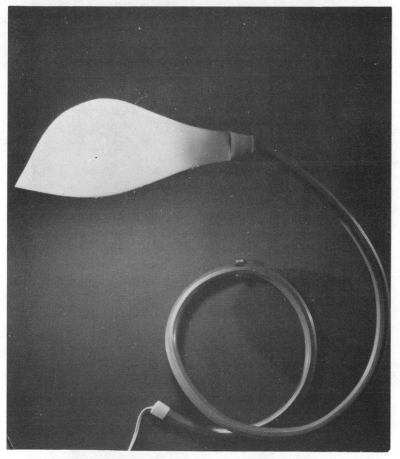

9   *The Bendalux Lamp, ideal for inspecting wines prior to bottling*

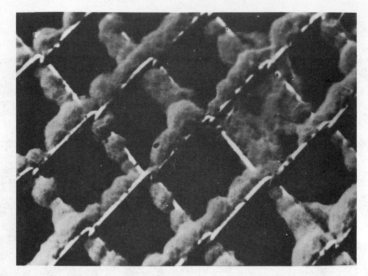

10   *Black Cellar Mould called Cladosporium cellare*

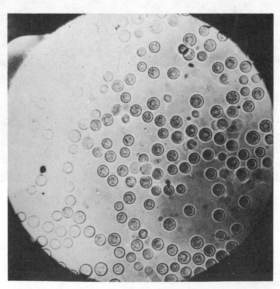

11   *Slime forming Torula*

9

Blending, Bottling and Storing Wines: The Wine Cellar

Wines may, even after some maturing, be found to be lacking in some way. They may be too high or too low in acid or tannin, or too dry or too sweet. Acid and tannin can be added of course even to the finished wine, but often better results are achieved by blending two or more wines together. This is done commercially too and in fact very many wines which are dull and unattractive can be vastly improved in this way. Blending of ingredients is sometimes carried out prior to fermentation, that is to say that acid fruits are mixed with those low in acid, or astringent fruits which often lack acid are mixed with less astringent but acid fruits. This is, for instance, the case when fermenting together grapes and elderberries, redcurrants and strawberries, cooking apples and crab apples. Such blending of ingredients is a reasonable approach, but many wine recipes advise such a hotchpotch of ingredients that the results can at no time be foreseen. By and large it is better to make the wines from single fruits and blend as skilfully as possible when the wines have received at least 6 to 9 months' maturing. To be able to blend well requires considerable experience of wines and of course a sensitive and trained palate. It cannot be too strongly emphasized that the more the winemaker attends commercial wine tastings or buys wines of quality the more competent will he become in assessing his own wines and improving them by blending. It may not generally be realized that both ports and sherries are, with a few exceptions such as vintage ports, wines which have undergone a considerable amount of blending. In fact, one of the most important tasks of a port shipper is to prepare a shipping lot, where many different ports are blended according to closely guarded recipes. Naturally, blending requires much tasting and even the most experienced taster, who spits out every mouthful he takes, will suffer from palate fatigue. He may have to defer his final assessment to another day. Wines freshly blended will not be at their peak of perfection until some weeks after bottling, as freshly bottled wines invariably suffer from 'bottle sickness'. This is one of the reasons why wines entered for showing so often fail. They are so often blended a few days before showing and will not be at their best until weeks later. When blending two or more dry wines together there is no danger of renewed fermentation, but when dry wines are blended with sweet ones the wine must be stored in bulk for at least a month to ensure that it is stable. The slightest haziness after blending is likely to be due to renewed yeast growth. It is wise to add a Campden or a Reductone tablet to the wine after blending as air uptake may also help to encourage renewed yeast growth.

When making Sherry type wines it is often necessary to sweeten a dry sherry a little. This is best done by adding a sweeter wine rather than a sweetened grape concentrate, as those available commercially are generally too acid. In Spain the concentrate used for sweetening is generally produced from very sweet but non-acid grapes. Many winemakers add sugar to their wines so as to render them a little less dry or even sweet. Such wines can easily start to ferment again and this method is not advocated if the wine is to be bottled at once. Nevertheless, if no sweet wine suitable for blending is available then sugar will have to be used and should be added by dissolving in some of the wine and mixing in. Such sweetened wine should be stored for a month to ensure that there is no further yeast growth and should on no account be sent to the show bench until it is certain that the wine is stable.

Bottling Wines. If the wine is brilliantly clear and stable it is ready for bottling. It is an astonishing thing that wines which are bottled and kept in cool conditions and protected by proper storage from air, should go on improving after bottling. That it does so is due to the fact that the alcohol in the wine combines with the acids present to form esters. There is no substitute for maturing, and when possible maturing in casks for six months to a year is particularly advantageous for full-bodied red wines rich in tannin. On the other hand the lighter and fruity white table wines require less maturing and appear to gain very little from being kept in cask, while they tend to improve on a year's storage in bottles.

Prior to bottling the wine must be inspected for clarity and freedom from deposit. The second inspection is of course easier if a glass container is used; and if wines are to be stored in a cask then it is as well to make a little more than fills the cask and store the excess in glass in the same place as the cask. If the wine is clear it can be syphoned straight into bottles. One gallon will fill six wine bottles. It is an advantage when bottling to use different types of bottles for the many types of wine made. The long hock bottles should be used for dry wines or very slightly sweet wines like some Rhine wines called Liebfraumilch. I keep the green bottles for dry grape wine and the brown ones for all other dry wines. Sweet white wines should be bottled in white or very pale green punted bottles and the latter are suitable for Rosé wines. All red wines should be put into dark green bottles, Ports in green or brown, Sherry in brown bottles and sparkling wines in heavy Champagne bottles. Chianti bottles, though attractive, are difficult to store and it is important that all wines excepting sherries are stored in a horizontal position so as to prevent the cork from drying out. Corking is not difficult but only the best quality, straight-sided corks should be used for dry and sweet table wines. Ports and Sherries may be corked with flanged corks. The corks are soaked in a cold 1 per cent Sulphite solution for 24 hours and must be kept covered with this solution. They can be weighted down and kept submerged with a plate. The solution is prepared by dissolving $\frac{1}{4}$ oz. of Potassium Metabisulphite (containing approximately 50 per cent of sulphite) in 12 ounces of water or adding 12 Campden tablets to half a pint of water. The corks are squeezed well in a clean linen cloth and then inserted into the bottles, using a proper corker. (Sanbri Corker—see Plate 2.)

Failing this the corks must be hammered into the bottle together with a thin wire or bit of string. Once the cork is driven home it must be held down and the wire or string withdrawn. This allows the air which has been compressed by the cork to escape. The wet cork will soon resume its shape in the bottle. If the wire had not been used the cork would be blown out by the compressed air. The bottles are next labelled and nothing is more useful than the Hartley garden label. It is best marked by pencil and if the larger size label is bought a hole can be pierced at the rounded end and after the label has been put round the neck of the bottle the point can be pushed into the hole and turned over. The labels can be used again and again by cleaning them with steel wool or an abrasive cleaning powder. Any other type of label will soon become illegible. The wines should next be stored in a cool dark place, the white wines in the cooler positions, the red wines a little warmer, that is higher up in the store. If any of the wines are to be used for showing then at least two white punted bottles should have been used as most show schedules make a point of exhibiting in such bottles. Also, if one bottle in the bin, that is in the section where a number of identical wines are stored, is white it enables the wines to be inspected from time to time.

Wine cellars are more or less a thing of the past, especially in this country, and it is not easy to find a suitable storage place for wines. Some ingenious winemakers have overcome this by taking up floorboards in a room without a fireplace and digging into the foundations. An outdoor concrete shed with an insulated roof which can remain a little moist is a very good compromise but failing that a dark cupboard in the coolest place in the house can be used. The cupboard should be kept dark as light tends to spoil a wine. Any ardent winemaker will consider the purchase of metal racks a necessity or else wooden shelves with several partitions will serve as wine bins. Where wines of the same kind are stored together it is only necessary to label one of the bottles, but where stored individually each bottle or row of bottles must be labelled. Wine bins can be supplied in any size and shape but for those who make wine in one or two gallons a rack with six divisions is a convenience.

Storage temperatures should be no lower than 45° F. or more than 55° F., but temperatures up to 60° F. may be allowed for Port type red wines. The latter wines should have the top of the bottle marked with a spot of white paint so that if any deposit is formed this is not disturbed by changing the position of the bottle. Recently a plastic wine bin, the 'Bottle Boy', has come on the market. It is most useful for transporting and storing wine. These containers open from the front, hold two dozen bottles, and can be stored on top of each other. All stored wines must be inspected from time to time.

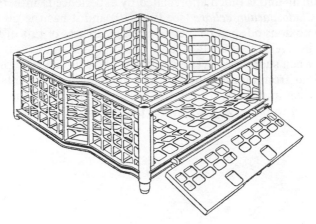

Plastic Storage Bin open empty

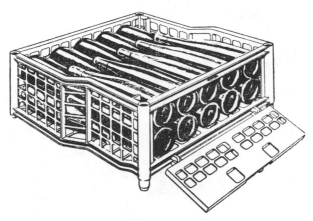

Plastic Storage Bin filled

Mould in Wine Cellars. Those who are the owners of damp wine cellars or concrete wine storage sheds may note that white flecks of mould appear on bottles and storage casks and bins. These moulds may eventually turn black and visitors to commercial cellars which have been used for many years will often find festoons of such moulds decorating barrels, containers and bins, and hanging from the ceiling. This mould has a lovely 'wine cellar smell' and is much appreciated by experienced vintners. It is called *Cladosporium cellare* (see Plate 10) and it has the power to absorb noxious odours, be they of rotting carcases of rats or wasps or rotting vegetable matter, and render them innocuous. This mould when supported over a container of garlic can even prevent this odour from tainting the air. As wines can absorb taints quite easily when in barrels, it is as well to appreciate the value of this mould and to preserve it whenever possible.

10

Wine and Food. The Serving of Wine

That wines vary in their nature is known to all consumers of wine. Naturally some wine drinkers prefer dry wines and other sweet wines, but the differences between various wines makes them particularly attractive with various foods. Let us consider wines which are consumed at the table. These range from very dry dinner wines such as the white Hocks, Moselles and Chablis to the red wines, the light Clarets, the Burgundies, the heavy Pommards and the Rosé wines. Fish generally calls for the more acid wines while with fowl or veal the more perfumed and less dry Hocks or even slightly sweet wines like the drier Graves or Liebfraumilch wines can be served. With red meats it is usual to serve red wines which are generally dry but sometimes have a trace of sweetness. The stronger flavoured the meat the better will it blend with a high tannin dark red wine. Wines suitable for consumption with fowl or cheese or egg dishes come in between a white and a red wine and are well served by Rosé wines slightly chilled. Red wines should be served at about 60° F., rather above than below this temperature. Red wines also are much better if they come to room temperature while the cork is removed to allow the wine to breathe and develop a better bouquet. This warming is called 'chambré'—what a beautiful, expressive and yet terse expression. It means 'at room temperature'. Three words are needed to translate chambré! Rosé wine can be served chilled or at room temperature. In general the more

71

acid the wine, the cooler the temperature at which it should be served. The most acid white wines are normally chilled at 53 to 54° F. and are particularly suitable for fish dishes. Although table wines are generally fairly low in alcohol the alcoholic flavour also becomes less obvious in a chilled wine. The sweeter dessert wines, like Sauternes and sweet Graves, are normally served at cellar temperature, that is about 50° F., while sweet after-dinner red or tawny Ports are better at room temperature; White Port which is somewhat similar to Sherry and consumed as an aperitive is, like Sherry, much improved by chilling. Sweet fortified wines such as Malaga or Madeira are generally not chilled but the drier Madeira is a wine which becomes more attractive if chilled. Champagne and other sparkling wines, be they white or red, dry or slightly sweet, have to be kept on ice so as to retain as much sparkle as possible. These wines can be served with any part of the meal and are generally kept for festive occasions. It is not usual to decant dinner wines but sometimes necessary in the case of older dark red wines, as they may easily have thrown a deposit. Such wines can be served rather more easily from a wine cradle or basket as there is less likelihood of disturbing the deposit. On the other hand Ports and particularly crusted Ports are generally decanted, and to ensure that the crust is not disturbed the cork is not drawn but the neck of the bottle is broken by placing heated tongs round the neck. This is often done by the wine merchant who decants the port into a fresh bottle.

Wine should be served in an elegant manner. The cap is removed and the cork is drawn by a good corkscrew. Then the bottle must be grasped as near to the base as possible, not round the neck, and the hand must be on top, not underneath the bottle. Serving like that not only ensures full control of the bottle but allows a quick twisting to the right before bringing the bottle upright. This will prevent drops of wine spilling and spoiling the tablecloth. Many wine waiters carry a napkin when serving red wines to wipe the outside of the bottle neck between each serving.

Wine bottles, particularly Ports, should be stood on special wine stands, also known as coasters. These are normally wooden stands with silver rims and felted bases and on polished tables they are 'coasted' along the table. Finally, a ritual is observed by most Port drinkers when dining; the wine is served in a decanter and passed round the table clockwise. The right hand neighbour serves the one on his left by holding the decanter in his right hand and filling the left-hand neighbour's glass, who in turn fills the glass on his left in a similar manner. Having experienced the hospitality of well-known Port shippers in Oporto, I was much impressed by this ritual and the beauty of dining and wining and imbibing some lovely ports by candlelight.

11

Wine Types and Your Cellar

In the previous chapter reference had been made to table, dessert, after-dinner and aperitive wines and champagnes. Such wines not only vary as to their sugar content and flavour but also in their alcohol content. The light dinner wines normally range in alcohol content from 9 to 13 per cent though sometimes the upper figure reaches a little higher; dessert wines from $13\frac{1}{2}$ to $15\frac{1}{2}$ per cent; while Ports and Sherries range from 17 to 22 per cent. Champagnes may contain anything from 10 to 12 per cent of alcohol. It is of course equally possible to prepare a similar range of wines from other fruits besides grapes. I purposely recommend fruits and flowers, rather than vegetables or cereals, as with such a wide range of fruits available I cannot see much justification for cereal or vegetable wines. Just as grapes can be used for all types of wines so can indigenous fruit be used for a range of wines. Grapes generally, with the exception of Muscat grapes, are rather nondescript in flavour and are therefore easier to use for a wide range of wines than say elderberries, blackcurrants or raspberries with their pronounced flavour. One has therefore to rely on experience and judgment to decide which fruits are more suitable for one type of wine than another. As the range of fruit is so wide it is easier to set out the suitability of various fruits in table form than to mention them separately.

74

TABLE II

INGREDIENTS SUITABLE FOR SPECIFIC WINE TYPES

A	B	C
DRY TABLE WINE WHITE also suitable for *CHAMPAGNE*	*DRY TABLE WINE RED* or *ROSÉ*	*SWEET DESSERT WINE WHITE SAUTERNE TYPE*
Average Sugar content 2–2½ lb per gallon	Average Sugar content 2–2½ lb per gallon	Average Sugar content 3½–4½ lb per gallon
Average Alcohol content from 9–14% by volume	Average Alcohol content from 9–14% by volume	Average Alcohol content from 13.5–15.5% by vol.
White Grape or Concentrate	Red Grape or Red Grape Concentrate	White Grape or White Grape Concentrate
Rhubarb	Elderberry & Grape	Apricot
Gooseberry, Green	Bilberry	Pineapple
Apricot	Loganberry	Peach
Grapefruit	Rose petal	Parsley
Pineapple	Hawthornberry	Orange
Orange	Redcurrant	Strawberry
Whitecurrant	Redcurrant & Blackcurrant	Apple
Peach		Pear
Nectarine	Plum	Rhubarb
Tangerine	Cranberry	
Elderflower	Wineberry	
Coltsfoot/Sultana	Strawberry	
Cowslip/Sultana	Sour Cherry	
Birch Sap		
Vine Prunings		

TABLE II (*continued*)

D	E
SWEET DESSERT WINE RED AND PORT TYPE	*SHERRY AND MADEIRA TYPE*
Average Sugar content 3½–5 lb per gallon by feeding method	Average Sugar content 3–5 lb per gallon by feeding method
Average Alcohol content 18–22% by volume	Average Alcohol content 17–21% by volume
Red Grape	White Grape
Elderberry	Rhubarb
Bilberry	Apple
Elderberry/Raisin	Strawberry
Prune/Elderberry	Rose Hip
Grape/Elderberry	Orange
Blackcurrant	Plum (not Damson)
Raspberry	Rowanberry
Damson	
Blackberry	

By and large dry dinner wines are made from fruit with as little flavour as possible, but some fruits are more suitable than others. Apart from grape or grape concentrate, for dry table wines I would choose whitecurrants, green gooseberries, grapefruit or apricots. Flowers such as coltsfoot and cowslip, with sultanas to help the fermentation, would be a subsequent choice, while birch sap juice, if properly balanced with acid and tannin, would also prove a useful starting point for a dry table wine. Apple juice does not easily make a white table wine, but if sufficiently sulphited and balanced with tannin can yield a superb Sauterne. For deep red table wines my first choice would be bilberries, fresh or dried, then elderberries blended with an acid fruit such as grapes or redcurrants. As the latter ripen long before elderberries, the wines would have to be fermented separately and blended, or dry elderberries could be used with redcurrants. Next a mixture of red and black currants make a good wine, and so do loganberries, especially if blended with a non-acid fruit like strawberries. Rose petals also give a fine light red or rosé wine and provided that sufficient sulphite is used, strawberries will be suitable for the production of rosé wines. All fruits which go brown very easily, such as

76

apples, pears, peaches, strawberries, plums, need larger than normal amounts of Campden tablets when used for table wines and are more particularly suitable for sherry-like wines. If it is desired to make Sauternes or similar sweet wines then the fruit content should be kept low so as to force the yeast to work under starving conditions and the sulphite content can be the maximum permitted, amounting to nine Campden tablets to the gallon. Also the full sugar content of 4 lb to the gallon should be added at the start of fermentation and the yeast helped to ferment against these odds by fermenting warm. All the fruits listed under C in Table II are able to yield wines similar to Sauternes if they are fermented under the stringent condition of a Sauterne fermentation. For a Sauterne wine I would definitely choose cooking apples rather than dessert apples and they should either be mixed with crab apples or half a teaspoonful of grape tannin should be added to the gallon.

Sweet unfortified red wines are not normally obtainable commercially in this country but they are sold in California. Domestically they can be made from bilberries, blackberries, elderberries and loganberries. They are the nearest approach to a port and they serve a useful function as a dessert wine or as a wine for drinking at any time. No doubt Port originally was a sweet red wine but as it tended to be unstable prior to exporting, alcohol was added to prevent renewed fermentation. Undoubtedly the most attractive wine of this type is made from bilberries closely followed by elderberries. These red fruits are all high in tannin content which is partly the reason for the attractiveness of the wines and a guide to the tannin content of fruits may prove of interest and a help in choosing fruits to produce a balanced must. The tannin content of all fruit varies with climate, variety and stage of ripening. For instance apples may range in tannin content from 0.05– to up to 1.2 per cent. This is mainly due to the variety of the apple as a crab apple is quite obviously much more astringent than a cooking or an eating apple. The tables on page 78 are therefore only a guide.

Reference to this table allows the winemaker to choose high tannin fruits for blending with rather insipid fruits, though the addition of grape tannin prior to fermentation can often be a useful alternative.

TABLE III*			TABLE IV†	
	Tannin %			Tannin %
Apples	0.5–1.2	Raspberries		0.07–0.14
Pears unpeeled	1.5	Redcurrants		0.06–0.13
Pears peeled	0.03	Blackcurrants		0.12–0.14
Quinces	0.07	Cherries sour		0.13–0.23
Mountain Ash	0.23	Cherries sweet		0.088
Plums	0.07	Strawberries		0.13
Greengages	0.17	Bilberries		0.09–0.20
Yellow Plums	0.15	Gooseberries		0.02–0.09
Cherries sweet	0.10	Cranberries		0.11–0.37
Cherries sour	0.18	Blackberries		0.13
Peaches whole	0.07	Mulberries		0.07–0.12
Grapes with skins	0.10	Peaches		0.12
Currants	0.21	Apples		0.07–0.30
Gooseberries	0.09	Pears		0.05–0.25
Cranberries	0.25	Quinces		0.12–0.46
Bilberries	0.22	Mountain Ash		0.29–0.87
Raspberries	0.26	Plums		0.05–0.20
Blackberries	0.29			
Strawberries	0.41			

Next we come to the aperitive Sherry-type wines. Here the choice of fruit is wide and those high in vitamin C tend to oxidize easily. Hips, oranges, ripe white gooseberries, raisins, apples, pears, apricots, peaches, purple or yellow plums and rhubarb contain vitamin C and all tend to brown quickly on exposure to air. They are particularly suitable for the production of sherry-like wines, and my choice would be more or less in order of listing. I think using grapes for home sherry production is too wasteful.

Champagnes or sparkling wines are mostly white and the juice of both white or red grapes or white grape concentrate, rhubarb or apricot can be used. Port-type dessert wines are best produced from the fruits suggested for sweet red wines and by having a high fruit content, about 6 lb to the gallon, by fermenting with a Port

* E. Hotter, *Chemical Composition of some Australian Fruits*, 1906.
† K. Windisch and Schmidt Z. 1909, 17, 584.

yeast with the addition of Yeast Energizer and by repeated addition of syrup a port quality can be achieved.

The foregoing lists should help the winemaker to devise an attractive collection of wines and set up a valuable cellar. Nevertheless it is desirable to restrict one's winemaking to a relatively few varieties as too many can cause quite unnecessary headaches. It cannot be too strongly emphasized that the bottles should be inspected every month or so in case a yeast deposit has formed.

12

Wine Recipes from A to Z

The following wine recipes will, for convenience, be arranged in alphabetical order. As many juices need the same treatment, the same recipe will not be repeated in full but reference will be made to the preceding recipe of a similar type. The section on Champagne will require more than a recipe and anyone making Champagne must be prepared to work with a hydrometer. The Table of Adjustment for Champagne (Table IV) suggests the use of strong sugar syrup; and just to remind the winemaker, this is produced from four pounds of sugar dissolved in 2 pints of boiling water. This will make four pints and therefore each pint will contain 1 lb of sugar. Another fact worth knowing is that each pound of sugar added to any liquid will increase the volume of the liquid by half a pint. If one therefore wants to have two pounds of sugar *in* a gallon it will necessitate the addition of the sugar to seven pints of juice to produce a gallon. For making the wine more acid, either citric or tartaric acid should be used. I prefer the former. It is a convenience and a help to accuracy to dissolve 4 oz of citric acid in some hot water and make this solution up to 8 oz. Then double the amount given in the recipes must be used i.e. 1 tablespoonful of solid (equivalent to $\frac{1}{2}$ oz in weight) will be equivalent to 1 oz of the solution of citric acid. Another point to remember; it will need from 15 to 20 times as much lemon juice as citric acid, or, in other words, for every teaspoonful of citric acid, allow 2 oz of lemon juice. This figure can only be approximate as the acid content of lemon juice varies. A final fact may be worth remembering and prove helpful to the winemaker; every 5 ounces of sugar added to each gallon of juice will increase the gravity of that juice by 10 degrees. Therefore 1 lb of sugar added to one gallon will increase the gravity by 32 degrees, but 1 lb of sugar *in the gallon* of juice will produce a gravity of 37.5 degrees or near enough 40. For those who want to work with the hydrometer, the starting gravities of dry wines should range from 75 to 95, and of semi-sweet and sweet wines from 115 to 150.

Better wines are made if:

The fruit content is kept low;
Campden tablets are used;
The wines are racked at recommended intervals.

Recipes will be given in:

British measure   1 gallon =8 pints =160 oz; 1 pint =20 oz.
U.S.A. measure   1 gallon =8 pints =128 oz; 1 pint =16 oz.
Metric measure   5 litres (4½ litres =approx. 1 British gallon.)

Note. The Campden tablets mentioned in these recipes are the number to be added at the start of the fermentation. Extra tablets are required at racking time.

Almond Wine

This is really an almond flavoured wine and sultanas are used to produce the base wine.

	BRITISH	U.S.A.	METRIC
Minced Sultanas	2 lb	1½ lb	1 kilo
Sugar	2 lb	1½ lb	1 kilo
Grape tannin	½ teasp.	½ teasp.	½ teasp.
Citric acid	½ tablesp.	½ tablesp.	½ tablesp.
Campden tablets	1	1	1
Yeast Energizer	½ teasp.	½ teasp.	½ teasp.
All Purpose wine yeast			
Water up to	1 gallon	1 gallon	5 litre

Ferment on the pulp for 2 to 3 days, stirring twice daily, using an All Purpose yeast. Strain, make up to 1 gallon, insert airlock and ferment on. When fermentation ceases, add 1 oz crushed bitter almonds which have been boiled with 3 to 4 oz of water. Leave the wine until clear and rack as required.

Wine Recipes from A to Z

Apple Wine Sweet

Dry Apple Wine is not particularly attractive but a sweet wine fermented with a Sauterne yeast can be quite like a Sauterne in character. Mince 8 lb of apples, preferably a mixture of cooking, dessert and crab apples, add at once 2 crushed Campden tablets to the pulp and press out juice. Add a little water to the pulp and press again. This should result in about 4 to 5 pints of juice.

	BRITISH	U.S.A.	METRIC
Apples	8 lb	6 lb	4 kilo
Campden tablets	2	2	2
Yeast Nutrient	½ teasp.	½ teasp.	½ teasp.
Sugar	2½–3 lb	1 lb 10 oz–2¼ lb	1¼–1½ kilo
Grape tannin (none if crab apples are used)			
if not—	1 teasp.	1 teasp.	1 teasp.
Sauterne yeast			
Water up to	1 gallon	1 gallon	5 litre

For a semi-sweet wine, reduce sugar by ½ lb or ¼ kilo.

Apricot Wine Dry or Sweet

Apricots are the most valuable of fruits for the production of dry table wines and sweet dessert wine. This fruit is rich in pectin which must be removed by treatment with a pectic enzyme as described on page 27. For dry wine use the smaller amount of fruit given in the recipe. If fresh fruit is used it must be peeled, the stones removed and blemishes cut out. Dried fruit is soaked and boiled until completely soft. A pressure cooker is useful.

	BRITISH	U.S.A.	METRIC
Fresh apricots or Dried Apricots	1 (or 2 lb)	¾ (or 1½ lb)	½ (or 1 kilo)
Boiling water	2 pint	2 pint	½ litre
Cold water	2 pint	2 pint	½ litre
Pectozyme	1 tablesp.	1 tablesp.	1 tablesp.
Sugar	½ lb	½ lb	¼ kilo
Yeast Energizer	1 teasp.	1 teasp.	1 teasp.
Campden tablets	1	1	1
All Purpose wine yeast			

82

Ferment on the pulp for 3 to 5 days. After straining add sugar for a dry or sweet wine.

Sugar	2 (or 3 lb)	1½ lb (or 2 lb 6oz)	1 (or 1½ kilo)
Citric acid	½ tablesp.	½ tablesp.	½ tablesp.
Grape tannin	1 teasp.	1 teasp.	1 teasp.
Water up to	1 gallon	1 gallon	5 litre

Apricot Pulp Wine Sweet (2 gallon)

	BRITISH	U.S.A.	METRIC
Tin of Apricot Pulp	1 lb 12 oz	1 lb 12 oz	¾ kilo
Pectozyme	1 heaped tablesp.	1 heaped tablesp.	1 heaped tablesp.
Yeast Energizer	1 teasp.	1 teasp.	1 teasp.
Citric acid	4 teasp.	3 teasp.	3 teasp.
Sugar	1 lb	¾ lb	½ kilo
Grape tannin	1—2 teasp.	1 teasp.	1 teasp.
Campden tablets	2	2	2

All Purpose wine yeast.

Pour 3 pints hot water over pulp, cool to blood heat, add all the above ingredients and ferment on pulp for 3 to 4 days. Strain, add 3 lb of sugar, 1 gallon of water, ferment on then add further sugar as required from 1 to 2 lb dissolved in water and make up 2 gallons.

Water up to	2 gallon	2 gallon	10 litre

Apricot Concentrate Wine—Recipe for 1 gallon of wine (semi-sweet)

    1 20 oz tin of Apricot Concentrate
    1 teaspoon Yeast Energizer
    1 teaspoon Pectinol
    4 lb Invert sugar
    8 tins or 160 oz of water
    1 Campden tablet (optional)
    Wine Yeast (previously prepared)

Mix all the ingredients with warm but not hot water, except the wine yeast, which should be added when the mixture has cooled to 75 degrees or less.

Rack off lees in 3 to 4 weeks, rack again in 2 months. Unless you feel it is necessary to sweeten the wine to taste, it should now be ready for bottling. Age for at least 6 months in the bottles. If extra sugar is added it should remain under fermentation locks until it is certain that fermentation is finished.

Recipe provided by Wine Art, Box 2701, Vancouver, B.C.

Aubergine (Egg plant) Wine

This fruit contains very little sugar and it is somewhat characterless. Peel, slice, cover with water, boil until soft and strain.

	BRITISH	U.S.A.	METRIC
Aubergine, white or purple	3 lb (about 8)	2 lb 6 oz	1½ kilo
Campden tablets	1	1	1
Yeast Nutrient	½ teasp.	½ teasp.	½ teasp.
Grape tannin	1 teasp.	1 teasp.	1 teasp.
Orange juice	1 pint	1 pint	½ litre
Citric acid	2 tablesp.	2 tablesp.	2 tablesp.
Sugar	2½ lb	2 lb	1¼ kilo
All Purpose wine yeast			
Water to	1 gallon	1 gallon	5 litre

Ferment on the pulp for two days, then strain and ferment on.

Banana Wine Sweet

Bananas are rich in starch and wines made from such substances sometimes do not become really clear. Luckily there are means of avoiding starch hazes, namely by using a yeast which attacks starch. This yeast ferments well and the wine will clear better than if fermented with the usual wine yeast.

	BRITISH	U.S.A.	METRIC
Mashed bananas	2 lb–3 lb	1½–2½ lb	1–1½ kilo
Sugar	2 lb	1½ lb	1 kilo
Campden tablets	1	1	1
Citric acid	1 tablesp.	1 tablesp.	1 tablesp.
Grape tannin	1 teasp.	1 teasp.	1 teasp.
Yeast Nutrient	½ teasp.	½ teasp.	½ teasp.
Make up to	5 pint	5 pint	3 litre

The fruit can be brought to boil with some of the water. The other ingredients are added after cooling.

Use a cereal wine yeast called Sacch. Oryza. Ferment on pulp 5 days.

| Strain, add sugar | 1–1½ lb | ¾–1 lb | ½–¾ kilo |
| Make up to | 1 gallon | 1 gallon | 5 litre |

Bees Wine

This seems to be of great interest to many winemakers and every now and then the cult of making Beeswine is revived; but then the big problem is finding a growth of these so-called 'Bees'. The best source is some country farmhouse, particularly in Yorkshire, but some yeast laboratories, such as the Brewing Foundation in Nutfield, Surrey, sometimes have supplies of this yeast. Known as *Saccharomyces pyriformis,* it tends to grow together with bacteria which causes the yeast to aggregate into lumps which rise up through the fermenting must to the surface. This is due to the gas which is held by these clumps and which on reaching the surface disengages and causes the lumps to sink down again. The method of feeding with small amounts of sugar also helps this movement as the sugar is not stirred in and the yeast will be fermenting at the bottom where the sugar concentration is highest. The clumps of yeast do look like busy little bees and this has caused this strange name. Sometimes they are called Palestine or California bees or Balm of Gilead. Sometimes the clumps tend to break down and the fermentation becomes an ordinary yeast fermentation with the yeast settling at the bottom. The phenomenon of clumping has been noted with ordinary wine yeast where the fermentation was slow in starting and probably the fruit contains lactic acid or other bacteria.

The Beeswine is made as follows: 2 oz of Demerara sugar are dissolved in a pint of cold water in a wide-mouthed jar such as a Kilner jar. Stand in a warm place, put in the 'bees' and keep covered with butter muslin. Add 1 teaspoon of ground ginger and 1 teaspoon of Demerara sugar daily for one week. Dissolve 3½ teacups of sugar in 4 teacups of boiling water, make up to 5 pints with cold water; add the juice of a large lemon. Strain the bees off through muslin and add the liquid to the syrup with stirring. Bottle in screw-topped Ginger Beer bottles but with stoppers resting in the bottle neck. Screw tight after 2 to 3 hours and leave 10 to 14 days before sampling. The 'bees' or the sediment is divided into half and used again as before.

Beetroot Wine (see text page 57)

	BRITISH	U.S.A.	METRIC
Beetroot	3–4 lb	2¼–3 lb	1½–2 kilo
Campden tablets	1	1	1
Grape tannin	1 teasp.	1 teasp.	1 teasp.
Sugar	2–3 lb	1½–2¼ lb	1–1½ kilo
Yeast Energizer	½ teasp.	½ teasp.	½ teasp.
Water up to	1 gallon	1 gallon	5 litre

Boil beetroot until soft, peel and pulp. Ferment on pulp for 5 days, stirring once daily. Use a Burgundy yeast.

Strain, make up again to a gallon and ferment on. A drier wine will require 1 lb less sugar.

Bilberry Wine

Undoubtedly this is the best fruit for the making of dry red wine or port-type wine. As the fruit has a very definite flavour it is desirable to use 2 Campden tablets to the gallon, otherwise the fruit flavour will remain very dominant. Bilberries are lacking in nutrient and vitamins so 1 teaspoon of Yeast Energizer is required to each gallon.

Bilberry Wine Dry

	BRITISH	U.S.A.	METRIC
Fresh bilberries	3–4 lb	2¼–3 lb	1½–2 kilo
Dried bilberries	½–1 lb	½–¾ lb	¼–½ kilo

Draw juice by pouring about 4 pints of boiling water over fruit, stir sugar into this, cool to blood heat before adding other ingredients.

Yeast Energizer	1 teasp.	1 teasp.	1 teasp.
Campden tablets	1	1	1
Citric acid	½ tablesp.	½ tablesp.	½ tablesp.

Grape tannin, not necessary
Sugar   2½ lb   2 lb   1¼ kilo
Burgundy or All Purpose yeast

Ferment on pulp for one week with stirring once daily. Press, make up to 1 gallon or 5 litre.

For *Bilberry Wine Sweet*, see Port-type wines.

Birch Sap Wine

Birch sap is an ideal bland juice for the making of wine. The trees should not be too young, a circumference of 30 inches is desirable. If the tree is tapped only once every two years and not more than a gallon is collected in March, it should not be harmed. A hole not more than ½ inch diameter and 1½ inches deep should be drilled into the tree, slanting up at an angle of 45 degrees. The distance from the ground should be convenient for collecting with a vessel, say from 18 to 24 inches. When a gallon has been collected the hole must be stopped with a wooden plug or dowel cut from a dowelling rod, which is held in position by a bandage until there is no further exudation of sap. The juice (which should have been kept covered all the time during collection, which may take up to three days) is now sweetened with about 2 lb of sugar and ½ lb minced sultanas to each gallon. The usual additions are made—1 tablespoon citric acid, or the juice of 3 to 4 lemons, some Grape Tannin, ½ teaspoon of Yeast Nutrient and a Campden tablet. More sugar is added if a sweet wine is required.

Blackberry

What a useful fruit is available just for the picking! It makes a lovely dry or sweet or sherry-type wine and in most cases the tannin content is high enough, so that none needs to be added. The recipe for dry and sweet wines applies also to Loganberry, Dewberry and Wineberry, but as Loganberries are more acid than Blackberries 1 lb less of fruit per gallon is used than in the case of Blackberries.

Blackberry Wine Dry

	BRITISH	U.S.A.	METRIC
Blackberries	3–4 lb	2¼–3 lb	1½–2 kilo
Pour boiling water over the fruit	4 pint	4 pint	2½ litre
Add sugar	2½ lb	2 lb	1½ kilo
and cold water	2 pint	2 pint	1 litre
Campden tablets	1	1	1
Yeast Nutrient	½ teasp.	½ teasp.	½ teasp.
Wine yeast or Sherry yeast			
Taste, add citric acid if lacking in acid.			
Add Pectozyme	½ tablesp.	½ tablesp.	½ tablesp.
Water up to	1 gallon	1 gallon	5 litre

Blackberry Wine Sweet

	BRITISH	U.S.A.	METRIC
Blackberries	4–6 lb	3–5 lb	2–3 kilo

Pour boiling water over fruit, then cool to blood heat. Other ingredients as for dry wine, but sugar to be added in two lots.

	BRITISH	U.S.A.	METRIC
Sugar	3½–4½ lb	2¾–3¼ lb	1¾–2¼ kilo
Pectozyme	1 tablesp.	1 tablesp.	1 tablesp.
Campden tablets	1	1	1
Water up to	1 gallon	1 gallon	5 litre

Ferment on pulp for 1 week, strain and ferment on.

Blackberry Shoot Wine

Gather the tips of brambles while young. Allow about 6 pints of tips (5″ long). Pour boiling water over this, strain. Add the juice of 4 oranges and 2 lemons, 1 Campden tablet, 1 teaspoon of Nutrient, 3½ lb of sugar, an All Purpose yeast and make up to the gallon. If desired 1 lb of minced sultanas can be added to each gallon.

Blackcurrant

This fruit is best for making a sweet red wine as the flavour is somewhat pronounced for a dry wine.

Wine Recipes from A to Z

Blackcurrant Wine Sweet

	BRITISH	U.S.A.	METRIC
Blackcurrants	3 lb	2¼ lb	1½ kilo
Boiling water to cover			
Sugar	3–4 lb	2¼–3 lb	1½–2 kilo
Cold water to cool to blood heat			
Campden tablet	1	1	1
Yeast Nutrient	½ teasp.	½ teasp.	½ teasp.
Pectozyme	1 tablesp.	1 tablesp.	1 tablesp.
All Purpose wine yeast			
Water up to	1 gallon	1 gallon	5 litre

Leave in warm airing cupboard for three days stirring twice daily. Strain, put into gallon jar and fill to top. Ferment on.

Broom Wine

Many flowers make delightful wines. The amount of blossom to use is 4 to 8 pints per gallon, with the exception of elderflowers and chamomile which are both rather pungent in flavour. Warm water is poured over the blossom, and ½ lb of minced sultanas are mixed in together with sugar, Campden tablets, citric acid, grape tannin and, when cool, Yeast Energizer and a wine yeast. For flower wines a Chablis yeast is recommended for dry wines and a Tokay yeast for sweet wines.

	BRITISH	U.S.A.	METRIC
Broom flowerheads	4–8 pint	4–8 pint	2–4 litre
Sultanas	½ lb	½ lb	¼ kilo
Sugar	2½–3½ lb	1 lb 14 oz–2 lb 10 oz	1¼–1¾ kilo
Campden tablets	1	1	1
Citric acid	3 teasp.	3 teasp.	3 teasp.
Yeast Energizer	½ teasp.	½ teasp.	½ teasp.
Grape tannin	½ teasp.	½ teasp.	½ teasp.
Water up to	1 gallon	1 gallon	5 litre

Ferment in presence of flowerheads for three days then strain and continue fermentation.

Wine Recipes from A to Z

Bullace Wine

This is a stone fruit like Apricot and Plum and should be treated with pectic enzyme. It is rather sour, so citric acid is not required.

	BRITISH	U.S.A.	METRIC
Bullaces	2–4 lb	1½–3 lb	1–2 kilo
Boiling water	2 pint	2 pint	½ litre
Cold water	2 pint	2 pint	½ litre
Pectozyme	1 tablesp.	1 tablesp.	1 tablesp.
Sugar	¼ lb	½ lb	¼ kilo
Yeast Energizer	½ teasp.	½ teasp.	½ teasp.
All Purpose wine yeast			
Water up to	1 gallon	1 gallon	5 litre

Ferment on the pulp for three to five days. After straining add sugar for a dry or sweet wine.

	BRITISH	U.S.A.	METRIC
Sugar	2 (or 3) lb	1½ (or 2½) lb	(1 or 1½) kilo
Campden tablet	1	1	1

Burgundy Type

Burgundy is a dry red grape wine but similar wines can be made from English fruits. The best fruits to use are a mixture of grapes and elderberries, 2 lb of each to the gallon, or bilberries 4–6 lb to the gallon or red and blackcurrants, 2 lb of red and 1 lb of black, or blackberries 4 lb to the gallon. The fruit is fermented on the pulp until colour is well extracted and not more than 2½ lb of sugar should be used per gallon. When grapes are used by themselves sugar required may be only one pound if the grapes are sweet. A Burgundy or Pommard yeast should be used.

Burnet Wine (as Broom Wine)

Carnation Wine (also Elderflower and Chamomile)

Carnation blossom, like elderflower and chamomile, is strongly scented and pungent. The wine is made similarly to Broom Wine (which see), but the amount of blossom used should be no more than 2 pints to the gallon.

Wine Recipes from A to Z

Carrot Wine

	BRITISH	U.S.A.	METRIC
Carrots	4 lb	3 lb	2 kilo
Sugar	2 lb	1½ lb	1 kilo
Sultanas, minced	1 lb	¾ lb	½ kilo
Yeast Energizer	1 teasp.	1 teasp.	1 teasp.
Grape tannin	½ teasp.	½ teasp.	½ teasp.
Campden tablets	1	1	1
Wine yeast			
Water up to	1 gallon	1 gallon	5 litre

Boil carrots until soft and strain off. Use the liquid to dissolve sugar, stir in sultanas and other ingredients and ferment to a dry wine.

Chamomile Wine (as Carnation Wine)

Champagne

True Champagne is produced in the Champagne district in northern France from the juice of a mixture of white and red grapes fermented to dryness in cask, chilled, clarified, fined, tested and blended. A predetermined amount of sugar is next added and the wine bottled, when renewed fermentation will ensue in the bottle. When all the sugar has been worked out the yeast is removed and the wine topped up if necessary with some stabilized and fortified sweet wine after which the bottle is recorked. The removal of the yeast requires some skill.

Amateurs can make such sparkling wines but they *must* follow directions closely if they want to *be successful and not incur danger from exploding bottles.*

First of all the base wine must be right and to ensure a satisfactory refermentation the starting gravity of the juice used after sweetening with cane sugar should be between 75 and 80. In Table IV the sugar additions required to produce a juice of this gravity are shown. The juice is tested first by putting it in a hydrometer jar, and a hydrometer spindle is lowered into the juice. The reading is taken and sugar added accordingly. Not more than 1 Campden tablet per gallon should be added and unless the juice is really sour 1 oz of citric acid is required to each gallon.

Juices suitable for making into sparkling wines are apple, pear, rhubarb, gooseberry and sultana. Any wine which has had a starting gravity of between 75 and 80 can be made into a sparkling wine.

TABLE IV

Sugar additions to achieve a gravity of 75 for juices to be made into a sparkling wine.

Gravity found in juice	To each gallon of juice add strong syrup*
5	2 pint 10 oz
10	2 pint 6 oz
15	2 pint 2 oz
20	1 pint 19 oz
25	1 pint 15 oz
30	1 pint 12 oz
35	1 pint 8 oz
40	1 pint 4 oz
45	1 pint 1 oz
50	17 oz
55	14 oz
60	10 oz
65	7 oz
70	3 oz

The juice adjusted to the right gravity is fermented to dryness.

An easy to make Champagne-type wine which can be produced all the year round is a Sultana Wine. One pound of sultanas is minced very finely and hot water poured over the fruit, 1 oz of citric acid and 1½ lb of white sugar are added and made up to 1 gallon. The gravity should be near enough 80. It is wise to take the gravity and adjust if necessary. A Champagne yeast and half a teaspoon of grape tannin, 1 teaspoon of Energizer and 1 crushed Campden tablet are next added. The fermentation should be conducted at about 70° F. (21° C.) in a wide-mouth vessel or polythene pail which is carefully covered with several layers of butter muslin. The juice is stirred twice daily and after 3 to 5 days is strained off through a coarse linen or hessian cloth. It is then

* Produced by adding 2 pints of boiling water to 4 lb of sugar. Each pint contains 1 lb of sugar.

transferred to a gallon jar full to the neck and fitted with an air-lock. When the fermentation has ceased the gravity must be below 1.00 and when the deposit has settled the wine is racked from the yeast into a clean jar and topped up with an ounce or two of water. Next the jar must be placed in the refrigerator as sultanas are dried grapes and contain cream of tartar. This has to be removed by chilling in all grape wines or in all cases where tartaric acid and a potassium salt have been added as a nutrient. After a week or so the wine will have deposited its cream of tartar and it has to be racked again. Now the wine is left to clear itself and finally it is fined.

After racking off following fining, some sugar is added to each gallon and a teaspoonful of Yeast Nutrient. The wine is left until a yeast deposit is noted which is then stirred up and the wine is bottled at once and firmly corked. The beginner is advised not to add more than 2 oz of sugar to the gallon of wine, and so gain his experience with a wine which has not too much pressure. Up to $3\frac{1}{2}$ oz can be used for higher pressures, or a method which gives even better results is to add 8 oz of sugar to the wine and when properly dissolved take the gravity. Now let the fermentation pro-ceed until very active, and when the gravity has dropped between 8 and 10 degrees, stir up the yeast deposit and bottle. The second fermentation in the bottle does not normally require the addition of fresh yeast but if the fermentation is a little sluggish then a tea-spoon of Yeast Energizer to the gallon is a help, i.e. about a pinch to a champagne bottle. Plastic, hollow corks can be used which are wired down. The bottles are laid on their sides in a temperate atmosphere (please note *not* warm) for 4 to 6 weeks. Then put into a cold shed for 6 to 12 months. The bottles should now be stored upside down and should be given a twisting shake once a week. If a wine carton is used do not lift the bottles too far out of the carton; and wear a glove. The yeast deposit should fall into the hollow cork and the wine should be put into the refrigerator for a day. Next the cork can be removed, still holding the bottle upside down. The wires are cut, the cork carefully edged out and the neck at once closed with the thumb and the bottle righted until the excess gas has blown off. With experience there should be little loss but the wine may be a little too dry. Top up with a sweetened wine which has been given a dose of Vodka (about 2 oz to 10 oz of wine, as it is important not to reduce the alcohol content of the Champagne). Insert a fresh solid plastic cork and wire this down.

It is not of course necessary to go to all the trouble of disgorging to produce a sparkling wine. Any yeast will render a wine sparkling, and if it is not intended to disgorge then a sticky yeast like an All Purpose yeast should be used. The second fermentation is again carried out in the bottle but not more than 2 oz of sugar should be added to each gallon of dry wine before bottling. The wine is chilled before serving and with careful pouring and keeping the bottle steady and not bringing it upright between serving, most of the wine can be poured without the yeast clouding the wine.

As mentioned in the beginning of this chapter any dry wine of low enough starting gravity can be used for turning into sparkling wine; and if the starting gravity was too high, say 120, then water can be added to the wine and the fermentation continued until the wine is dry. The amount is easily arrived at. If the gravity was 120 and you are looking for a starting gravity of 80, then 80 oz are made to 120 oz or 8 pints are made up to 12 pints. In other words to each gallon of wine add half a gallon of water *and* some more acid and tannin—half an ounce of citric acid and half a teaspoon of grape tannin.

Cherry Wine Dry and Sweet

The best cherries for wine making are sour Morello cherries, but provided that sufficient Campden tablets are used, black cherries make a lovely dry wine or sweet wine. Eating cherries are low in acid so this has to be added; and like other stone fruit they contain plenty of pectin, so the addition of Pectozyme and pulp fermentation is recommended.

The larger amounts of fruit and sugar are recommended for a sweet wine. No added acid is required for Morello cherries but ¾ oz of citric acid per gallon is required for dessert cherries together with 3 Campden tablets to the gallon.

	BRITISH	U.S.A.	METRIC
Cherries	3–5 lb	2¼–3¾ lb	1½–2½ kilo
Pectozyme	1 tablesp.	1 tablesp.	1 tablesp.
Citric acid if required	1–2 tablesp.	1–2 tablesp.	1–2 tablesp.
Yeast Nutrient	½ teasp.	½ teasp.	½ teasp.

Campden tablets	2–3	2–3	2–3
Sugar	2–4 lb	1½–3 lb	1–2 kilo
All Purpose wine yeast			
Water up to	1 gallon	1 gallon	5 litre

Cherry Concentrate Wine (Semi-sweet). Recipe for 1 gallon*

> 1 20 oz tin Cherry Concentrate
> 1 teaspoon Yeast Nutrient
> 1 teaspoon citric acid
> 3 lb invert sugar
> 7 tins or 140 oz of water
> Wine yeast
> 1 Campden tablet (optional)

This may be fermented in a 2-gallon plastic pail covered with a plastic sheet for 7 days, then syphoned into a gallon jar fitted with a fermentation lock.

Mix all the ingredients with warm water and when they have cooled to 70° F., add previously prepared wine yeast.

Rack off the sediment in 3 to 4 weeks, and top up with a sugar and water solution of a specific gravity of 100. Rack again in 2 months, sweeten if necessary to S.G. of 1.000 to 1.010. This wine should be clear and palatable in 3 to 5 months. Will continue to improve up to one year.

This recipe may be multiplied as many times as desired. The addition of ¼ teaspoon of grape tannin may improve the flavour for some tastes.

Warning.—Do not add wine yeast until temperature is down below 75° F.

Cider (from Apple Concentrate). Recipe for 1 gallon.*

> 1 20 oz tin of Apple Concentrate
> 1 teaspoon of Yeast Nutrient
> 1 teaspoon of citric or malic acid
> 8 tins or 160 oz of water
> 1 Campden tablet
> ¼ teaspoon grape tannin (optional)
> Champagne yeast

If you are making 1 gallon only it may be fermented in a

* By courtesy of Messrs Wine Art, Vancouver, B.C.

2-gallon pail covered with a plastic sheet. Mix all the ingredients except the yeast in warm water, and when cooled to 75° F. add the wine yeast and allow to ferment until all of the natural sugar is gone or the specific gravity reaches .998. Then syphon into a clean container, add 2 oz of sugar to the total volume of cider and bottle in beer bottles with crown caps.

Keep for three months and drink as Champagne cider.

If a slightly sweet cider is desired add 2 to 4 quarter grain sucaryl tablets to the gallon immediately prior to bottling.

This recipe may be multiplied as many times as desired.

Cider

This beverage is not a wine but a very refreshing sparkling drink of low or medium alcohol content. The best ciders are made from proper cider apples high in tannin and low in acid, but failing these a mixture of one part of crab apples, one of cooking apples and one of dessert is suitable for the production of a satisfactory cider. The fruit is milled or minced, at once sulphited with 4 tablets to 15 lb of fruit, and the pulp is left in a covered vessel over-night. The next day the juice is pressed out using a coarse hessian bag. The pulp is mixed with 2 pints of water and repressed, an All Purpose yeast and 1 teaspoon Yeast Nutrient should be added and the juice left to ferment. The volume of the juice will be between 7 and 8 pints. Put 6 pints in the gallon jar and 2 pints into a smaller container. When the fermentation slows down the gallon jar is filled from the smaller vessel. The usual airlock is of course required. After the yeast and debris has settled, the cider is racked, about 4 oz of sugar are added, and the container filled up to the top. A very slow second fermentation will resume and more yeast will settle out. The cider can be racked after another 3 months. It is tasted and citric acid and grape tannin are added if necessary. If not brilliantly clear the cider should be fined. After this 2 oz of sugar are dissolved in some of the cider and then mixed with the bulk and the cider can be bottled. It will go sparkling on storage. For those who like a slightly sweet cider 20 saccharin tablets can be added to the gallon before bottling.

Clove Wine

Allow about 1 oz of bruised cloves to 1 gallon. This and the thin rind of 2 oranges is put into a muslin bag and simmered in a few pints of water for 15 to 20 minutes. The juice only of the fruit is used.

	BRITISH	U.S.A.	METRIC
Cloves	1 oz	1 oz	25 gram
Oranges	4 large	4 large	4 large
Lemons	3 large	3 large	3 large
Sugar	3 lb	2¼ lb	1½ kilo
Campden tablets	1	1	1
Yeast Energizer	½ teasp.	½ teasp.	½ teasp.
Water up to	1 gallon	1 gallon	5 litre

This wine is particularly useful for liqueurs.

Clover Wine (as Broom Wine)

Coltsfoot Wine (as Broom Wine)

Cowslip Wine (as Broom Wine)

Instead of sultanas 2 pints of grape concentrate could be used for each gallon, but in this case the wine must be chilled prior to bottling to remove crystals of cream of tartar.

Cranberry Wine

	BRITISH	U.S.A.	METRIC
Cranberries	4–6 lb	3–4½ lb	2–3 kilo
Sugar	4 lb	3 lb	2 kilo
Campden tablets	1	1	1
Yeast Nutrient	½ teasp.	½ teasp.	½ teasp.
Burgundy wine yeast			
Water up to	1 gallon	1 gallon	5 litre

Wash the fruit then pour sufficient boiling water over it to cover, mash, add the sugar and stir to dissolve. Make up to volume with cold water and add the nutrient, Campden tablets and the yeast. Ferment on the pulp for a few days then strain and ferment on.

Wine Recipes from A to Z

Currant Wine

Currants, raisins and sultanas contain about 60 per cent extractable sugar but are low in acid and require the addition of a vitamin yeast food such as Yeast Energizer.

	BRITISH	U.S.A.	METRIC
Currants minced	2 lb	1½ lb	1 kilo
Sugar	1½ lb	1 lb 2 oz	¾ kilo
Yeast Energizer	½ teasp.	½ teasp.	½ teasp.
Citric acid	4 teasp.	4 teasp.	4 teasp.
Grape tannin	½ teasp.	½ teasp.	½ teasp.
Campden tablets	2	2	2
Sherry or Tokay yeast			
Water up to	1 gallon	1 gallon	5 litre

Pour some boiling water over the minced fruit and beat well into the pulp. Add the remainder of the water, preferably luke-warm, sugar and other ingredients. Ferment on the pulp for 2 to 3 days, strain and ferment on.

Cyser

This is made from apple juice and honey and can be either dry or sweet. One to two pounds of crab apples are minced and the juice strained off. The juice added to ½ gallon water in which from 3 to 4 lb of honey have been dissolved makes an attractive wine with the usual addition of acid and Yeast Nutrient and a wine yeast.

	BRITISH	U.S.A.	METRIC
Crab apples minced	1–2 lb	¾–1½ lb	½ kilo
Honey	3–4 lb	2¼–3 lb	1½–2 kilo
Yeast Nutrient	½ teasp.	½ teasp.	½ teasp.
Citric acid	1 tablesp.	1 tablesp.	1 tablesp.
Campden Tablets	2	2	2
Wine Yeast			
Water up to	1 gallon	1 gallon	5 litre

Dandelion Wine (as Broom Wine)

Damson Wine

	BRITISH	U.S.A.	METRIC
Damson	2–4 lb	1½–3 lb	1–2 kilo
Sugar	2½–4 lb	1¾–3 lb	1¼–2 kilo
Pectozyme	1 tablesp.	1 tablesp.	1 tablesp.

Yeast Nutrient	½ teasp.	½ teasp.	½ teasp.
Campden tablets	1	1	1
Burgundy yeast			
Water up to	1 gallon	1 gallon	5 litre

Pour 2 pints of boiling water on the fruit, using the smaller quantity for a dry wine, add 1 lb of sugar, 2 pints of cold water, and the pectic enzyme and yeast. Leave in a warm cupboard 1 to 2 days. Strain off, add the balance of the sugar, 1½ lb for dry wine, 3 lb for a sweet wine and Yeast Nutrient. Make up to a gallon and add 2 crushed Campden tablets. Ferment on. If the dry wine appears rather harsh add 5 oz of glycerin to the gallon of wine.

Date Wine

Dates, like currants, contain about 60 per cent of sugar. The dates are disintegrated in hot water and the juice balanced with acid and tannin, both of which are lacking in dates.

	BRITISH	U.S.A.	METRIC
Dates	3 lb	2¼ lb	1½ kilo
Sugar	1–2 lb	¾–1½ lb	½–1 kilo
Citric acid	2 tablesp.	2 tablesp.	2 tablesp.
Grape tannin	1 teasp.	1 teasp.	1 teasp.
Campden tablets	1	1	1
Yeast Energizer	½ teasp.	½ teasp.	½ teasp.
Sherry yeast			
Water up to	1 gallon	1 gallon	5 litre

Dewberry Wine (as Blackberry)

Elderberry Wine

The elderberry is really the most useful fruit for the winemaker and in particular sweet wines made from elderberries can be really delicious.

This fruit lends itself also to the making of a Burgundy-type wine and for this 3 lb of fruit and 1 lb of minced sultanas with about 1 tablespoon of citric acid, to balance the high tannin content of the elderberry, will produce a fine wine on maturing. The addition of 5 oz of glycerin to the gallon of the finished wine helps.

99

Wine Recipes from A to Z

Elderberry Wine Dry

	BRITISH	U.S.A.	METRIC
Elderberries	3 lb	2⅓ lb	1½ kilo
Sultanas minced	1 lb	¾ lb	½ kilo
Sugar	2 lb	1½ lb	1 kilo
Citric acid	1 tablesp.	1 tablesp.	1 tablesp.
Yeast Nutrient	½ teasp.	½ teasp.	½ teasp.
Campden tablets	1	1	1
All Purpose wine yeast or Pommard yeast			
Water up to	1 gallon	1 gallon	5 litre

Strip the fruit from the stems and weigh, then boil with water, and strain. Add the sultanas and sugar, make up to 1 gallon and add the 1 Campden tablet, citric acid, nutrient and yeast. Ferment on.

Elderberry Wine Sweet

	BRITISH	U.S.A.	METRIC
Elderberries	4 lb	3 lb	2 kilo
Sultanas	1 lb	¾ lb	½ kilo
Sugar	3½ lb	2½ lb	1¾ kilo
Citric acid	1 tablesp.	1 tablesp.	1 tablesp.
Yeast Nutrient	½ teasp.	½ teasp.	½ teasp.
Campden tablets	1	1	1
All Purpose yeast			
Water up to	1 gallon	1 gallon	5 litre

Method as above.

Elderberry Wine Port-type

	BRITISH	U.S.A.	METRIC
Elderberries	6–8 lb	4½–6 lb	3–4 kilo
Sugar	4–5 lb	3–4 lb	2–2½ kilo
Citric acid	1 tablesp.	1 tablesp.	1 tablesp.
Yeast Nutrient	1 teasp.	1 teasp.	1 teasp.
Campden tablets	1	1	1
Port yeast			
Water up to	5 pint	5 pint	2½ litre

Method. Pour boiling water over fruit, dissolve 1 lb sugar in this, add cold water and when lukewarm the other ingredients and yeast. Ferment to dryness. It will be very rough in taste but now the wine has to be fermented on with up to another 3 to 4 lb of sugar. This is done by dissolving 4 lb of sugar in 2 pints of boiling water. It will make 4 pints of syrup. One pint is added to the dry wine and fermented on. This is repeated with the second pint and followed by the third and, if not sweet enough, by the fourth pint. The wine can become quite strong and must not be racked for a month after the fermentation has ceased. Then it is syphoned off the deposit and the container filled bung full with some of the remaining syrup. It must be left at least another 3 months and racked again. If too sweet then it means that the alcohol content is not as high as it could have been so about 5 oz of 140 proof Vodka should be added to each gallon. The wine need not be racked again after the addition of the alcohol and perhaps after a year it will go tawny. It may then be bottled.

Elderflower Wine (as Carnation Wine)

Many consider Elderflower Wine one of the loveliest of wines while others loathe the taste. This is no doubt due to the fact that some use, at the utmost, one pint of the flowers while others use at least four times as much. Be that as it may, certainly the scent of elderflowers can make a dull flavourless wine more attractive and it is reputed that in some winemaking districts of Germany the flowers were used in small quantities to confer some bouquet on dull wines.

The flowers can be fermented on their own with some orange and lemon juice and nutrients or they can be made into wine with the help of minced sultanas as in Carnation Wine.

Fig Wine

Figs, strange as it may seem, belong to the mulberry family. Both dried and fresh figs can be used for winemaking. The fruit is extremely low in acid and two tablespoons or 1 oz of citric acid must be added to each gallon. Sugar in the fresh fruit averages 10 per cent though it has on occasion reached 15 per cent. Allow 6 lb of the fresh fruit or $1\frac{1}{2}$ to 2 lb of the dried fruit to the gallon and one tablespoon of pectic enzyme. The dried fruit has to be extracted with hot water and a yeast energizer added while the fresh fruit is mashed and yeast nutrient suffices.

	BRITISH	U.S.A.	METRIC
Figs, dry	1½–2 lb	1–1½ lb	¾–1 kilo
or			
Figs, fresh	6 lb	4½ lb	3 kilo
Sugar	2–3 lb	1½–2¼ lb	1–1½ kilo
Pectozyme	1 tablesp.	1 tablesp.	1 tablesp.
Yeast Energizer			
or Nutrient	½ teasp.	½ teasp.	½ teasp.
Citric acid	2 tablesp.	2 tablesp.	2 tablesp.
Campden tablets	1	1	1
Grape tannin	½ teasp.	½ teasp.	½ teasp.
Sherry yeast			
Water up to	1 gallon	1 gallon	5 litre

Ginger Wine

	BRITISH	U.S.A.	METRIC
Ginger root, bruised	2 oz	2 oz	60 gram
Orange juice	10 oz	8 oz	300 gram
Lemon juice	4 oz	3 oz	100 gram
Citric acid	1 tablesp.	1 tablesp.	1 tablesp.
Sultanas, minced	1 lb	¾ lb	½ kilo
Sugar	2–3 lb	1½–2¼ lb	1–1½ kilo
Yeast nutrient	½ teasp.	½ teasp.	½ teasp.
Grape tannin	1 teasp.	1 teasp.	1 teasp.
Campden tablets	1	1	1
All Purpose wine yeast			
Water up to	1 gallon	1 gallon	5 litre

The ginger is well bruised and a few pints of boiling water are poured over the root and gently simmered for half an hour. Strain, add the cold water and other ingredients and make up to 1 gallon. Ferment on.

Golden Rod Wine (as Broom)

Wine Recipes from A to Z

Gooseberry Wine Dry

	BRITISH	U.S.A.	METRIC
Green unripe gooseberries	2 lb	1½ lb	1 kilo
Sugar	2½ lb	2 lb	1¼ kilo
Pectozyme	1 tablesp.	1 tablesp.	1 tablesp.
Yeast Nutrient	½ teasp.	½ teasp.	½ teasp.
Campden tablets	1	1	1
All Purpose or Champagne yeast			
Water up to	1 gallon	1 gallon	5 litre

The gooseberries are chopped and about 4 pints of boiling water are poured over the fruit. The sugar is stirred in and the juice made up to 1 gallon with tepid water. The juice must be warm but not hot, the Pectozyme is added followed by Yeast Nutrient and a suitable yeast. The fermentation vessel is next placed in a warm airing cupboard and stirred several times a day. After two days the pulp may be strained off and the fermentation continued in a gallon jar fitted with an airlock. This wine will be suitable for making into a sparkling wine by re-fermenting after bottling (see Champagne).

Gooseberry Wine Sweet

	BRITISH	U.S.A.	METRIC
Red ripe gooseberries	3–4 lb	2½–3 lb	1½–2 kilo
Sugar	3–4 lb	2½–3 lb	1½–2 kilo
Pectozyme	1 tablesp.	1 tablesp.	1 tablesp.
Yeast Nutrient	½ teasp.	½ teasp.	½ teasp.
Campden tablets	2	2	2
Malaga yeast			
Water up to	1 gallon	1 gallon	5 litre

About 4 pints of boiling water are poured over the fruit which must *be sound and free from split berries*, and the fruit is mashed. 1 lb of sugar is stirred in and cold water added until tepid. The Nutrient, Campden tablets and yeast are added and this mixture is kept in a warm airing cupboard with twice daily stirring for 5 or 6 days. It is then strained and another 2 lb of sugar added dissolved either in the juice or in the minimum of boiling water. When fermentation ceases the wine is tasted and more sugar added if necessary and the volume made up to 1 gallon and fermented on.

Gorse Wine (as Broom Wine)

Grape Wine

This is fully described in Chapter 3 as the Wine of Wines. The wine types described were dry white and dry red wines. Sweet wines can also be made from grapes, but as this juice ferments very well it is better to add the extra sugar required for a sweet wine all at once and not in several stages. If feeding is resorted to there will be a tendency for the production of too much alcohol and the wine would lack quality. For a Sauterne-type wine the grape juice will have to be brought up to a gravity of 140 to 150. This is achieved by the addition of $2\frac{1}{4}$ to $3\frac{1}{2}$ lb of sugar to each gallon of juice of an approximate gravity of between 40 to 60. This is the gravity which may be expected in outdoor grapes grown in this country, but it is wiser to use a hydrometer to make sure and then add 5 oz of sugar to a gallon to increase the gravity by 10. If the juice has a gravity of 50 and 140 is desired then the difference $140-50 =90$ means that 9×5 oz have to be added to each gallon to bring the gravity up to 140, i.e. 2 lb 13 oz.

Sweet red wines can be made in a similar manner but the commercial equivalents—the Ports—retain their sugar content by the addition of alcohol to stop the fermentation while there is still sugar present. This is too costly a proposition for the amateur. Nevertheless something resembling a port wine can be made by fermenting red grapes with repeated additions of sugar which are stirred into the must. This produces maximum alcohol content and, with the addition of extra tannin, the wine can become very port-like in character. (See also Elderberry Wine, Port type).

Grape Concentrate Wine

Grape Concentrate of good quality is available in 1 lb tins which are each sufficient to make 1 to 2 gallons of dry wine when diluted with water and sweetened to a desirable gravity. The usual additions of Campden tablets and Grape tannin are needed and as the concentrate will be lacking in vitamins a Yeast Energizer should be used rather than a nutrient. Sometimes citric acid is also required. The wine must be chilled prior to bottling in case cream of tartar has not been thrown out.

	BRITISH	U.S.A.	METRIC
Grape Concentrate, red or white	1–2 lb	¾–1½ lb	½–1 kilo
Sugar	1 lb	¾ lb	¼ kilo
Grape tannin	1 teasp.	1 teasp.	1 teasp.
Yeast Energizer	½ teasp.	½ teasp.	½ teasp.
Campden tablets	1	1	1
All Purpose wine yeast			
Water up to	1 gallon	1 gallon	5 litre

Grapefruit Wine (as Orange Wine. See Chapter 2)

Greengage Wine

	BRITISH	U.S.A.	METRIC
Greengages	2–4 lb	1½–3 lb	1–2 kilo
Pectozyme	1 tablesp.	1 tablesp.	1 tablesp.
Sugar	2½–4 lb	2–3 lb	1¼–2 kilo
Grape tannin	1 teasp.	1 teasp.	1 teasp.
Campden tablets	1	1	
Yeast Nutrient	½ teasp.	½ teasp.	½ teasp.
All Purpose wine yeast			
Water up to	1 gallon	1 gallon	5 litre

Use the smaller quantity of fruit and sugar for a dry wine, the larger for a sweet wine and for a semi-sweet wine 3¼ lb of sugar suffices. Pour boiling water over the ripe but sound fruit, stir in 1 lb of sugar followed by an equal quantity of cold water, then add the other ingredients including the yeast and leave in a covered plastic pail for three days in a warm airing cupboard. Stir twice daily and at the end of three days the plums should be completely free from sliminess and easy to strain. If not, leave for another day or two. Strain through a coarse hessian cloth or bag, add the rest of the sugar, make up to 1 gallon and ferment on. The fermentation may take a day or two to get going again.

Guava Wine (4 gallons)

18 lb fruit
3½ gallons water
7½ lb white sugar
3 teaspoons citric acid
3 lemons
3 teaspoon Yeast Nutrient

Top and tail fruit, boil and strain. Allow to cool. Add all other ingredients, use All Purpose wine yeast. This wine requires racking about three times, takes fourteen months to clear, is amber in colour. A very nice bouquet and makes an excellent table wine. ½ fluid ounce syrup must be added to each wine bottle. Tightly cork. Semi-sweet wine.

Recipe by courtesy of Mr T. Ward, Salisbury, Southern Rhodesia.

Author's Note: Generally in this country it is wise to consume the wine soon after adding syrup, but where the fermentation and maturing have been carried out in a warmer climate the wine may be stable enough for sweetening.

Hawthorn Flower Wine (as Broom Wine)

Hawthornberry Wine

	BRITISH	U.S.A.	METRIC
Hawthornberries	4 pints	4 pints	2 litre
Sugar	2¼–3½ lb	2–3 lb	1¼–1½ kilo
Minced sultanas	1 lb	¾ lb	½ kilo
Citric acid	2 tablesp.	2 tablesp.	2 tablesp.
Campden tablets	2	2	2
Yeast Energizer	½ teasp.	½ teasp.	½ teasp.
Sherry yeast			
Water up to	1 gallon	1 gallon	5 litre

Bring the fruit to boil with 6 pints of water, add the sugar and minced sultanas. Make up to 1 gallon with cold water, add Yeast Energizer, citric acid and Sherry yeast. Leave to ferment.

Hock-type Wine

Hock is a dry white grape wine, of medium alcohol content.

Any dry white wine which is not too high in alochol and not too predominant in fruit and flower flavour can be like a Hock. This is best made from white currants, gooseberries, rhubarb, pears or apricots. The wines can be very similar to Hocks, especially after maturing for a year when the predominant fruit flavour will have disappeared.

Honey Wine (see Mead)

Hypocras (Hippocras) (see Mead)

Lemon Wine

	BRITISH	U.S.A.	METRIC
Lemons	10	10	10
Sugar	3 lb	2½ lb	1½ kilo
Sultanas, minced	1 lb	¾ lb	½ kilo
Yeast Nutrient	½ teasp.	½ teasp.	½ teasp.
Campden tablets	1	1	1
All Purpose wine yeast			
Water up to	1 gallon	1 gallon	5 litre

Thinly pare the rind of the lemons and cover with 4 pints of hot water. Add the juice of the lemons, sugar and nutrient, make up to 1 gallon, add the wine yeast and ferment on.

Lime Wine (as Lemon)

Litchi Wine

	BRITISH	U.S.A.	METRIC
Litchies	8 lb	6 lb	4 kilo
Citric acid	¾ tablesp.	¾ tablesp.	¾ tablesp.
Pectozyme	1 tablesp.	1 tablesp.	1 tablesp.
Grape tannin	½ teasp.	½ teasp.	½ teasp.
Yeast Nutrient	½ teasp.	½ teasp.	½ teasp.
Sugar	3½ lb	3 lb	1¾ kilo
Campden tablets	1	1	1
All Purpose wine yeast			
Water up to	1 gallon	1 gallon	5 litre

Remove the stones. Pour about 4 pints of boiling water over the

107

pulp. Stir in 1 lb of sugar and when at about 30° C. add the other ingredients with the exception of the remainder of the sugar. Keep in a warm airing cupboard for two days with stirring, strain and dissolve the rest of the sugar in water and make up to 1 gallon. Ferment on.

Loganberry Wine (as Blackberry Wine but requires less added citric acid and only 3 lb of fruit per gallon).

Loquat Wine (4 gallons)

> 16 lb fruit
> 3 gallons water
> 6 lb 12 oz white sugar
> 3 lemons
> 3 teaspoons citric acid
> 2 teaspoons Yeast Nutrient

Top and tail fruit, remove stones, boil, strain the fruit. When cold add all ingredients. Use All Purpose wine yeast. Should be bottled at eight months. Rack about three times—makes a beautiful clear dinner wine. One fluid ounce syrup should be added to each bottle when bottling.

Recipe by courtesy of Mr T. Ward, Salisbury, Southern Rhodesia.

Author's Note: Generally in this country it is wise to consume the wine soon after adding syrup but where the fermentation and maturing have been carried out in a warmer climate the wine may be stable enough for sweetening.

Madeira-type Wines

Madeira, a dark rich and expensive wine, is made from a grape wine which is aged and altered by being kept at elevated temperatures for several months. Orange juice, rose-hips, raisins or sultanas fermented with a Madeira yeast and Demerara sugar can be somewhat liqueury in flavour and resemble Madeira. It is suggested that Campden tablets be omitted and the fermenter left open to the air but protected by a cotton wool plug or butter-muslin, that the fruit content be high, a Yeast Energizer used and the sugar added at intervals—not all at once.

Wine Recipes from A to Z

Maize Wine

The author is not much in favour of cereal wines as generally they are potent but lacking in flavour and vinosity. Some people state that they make whisky from maize or wheat, but that is hardly possible. It is usual to add some minced sultanas or raisins to the kibbled maize, and also it is best to use a special yeast which attacks the starch.

	BRITISH	U.S.A.	METRIC
Maize, crushed	1 lb	$\frac{3}{4}$ lb	$\frac{1}{2}$ kilo
Sultanas, minced	1 lb	$\frac{3}{4}$ lb	$\frac{1}{2}$ kilo
Sugar	3 lb	$2\frac{1}{2}$ lb	$1\frac{1}{2}$ kilo
Orange juice	4 oz	3 oz	100 ml.
Citric acid	2 tablesp.	$1\frac{1}{2}$ tablesp.	2 tablesp.
Yeast Energizer	$\frac{1}{2}$ teasp.	$\frac{1}{2}$ teasp.	$\frac{1}{2}$ teasp.
Grape tannin	1 teasp.	1 teasp.	1 teasp.
Campden tablets	1	1	1
Cereal wine yeast and a Tokay yeast			
Water up to	1 gallon	1 gallon	5 litre

Pour boiling water over fruit and maize. Stir in sugar add cold water and make up to 1 gallon after adding the other ingredients.

Mangold Wine (as Beetroot)

Marrow Wine

	BRITISH	U.S.A.	METRIC
Marrow	4 lb	3 lb	2 kilo
Pectozyme	1 tablesp.	1 tablesp.	1 tablesp.
Citric acid	2 tablesp.	2 tablesp.	2 tablesp.
Yeast Nutrient	$\frac{1}{2}$ teasp.	$\frac{1}{2}$ teasp.	$\frac{1}{2}$ teasp.
Campden tablets	1	1	1
Grape tannin	1 teasp.	1 teasp.	1 teasp.
Sugar	$2\frac{1}{2}$–$3\frac{1}{2}$ lb	2–3 lb	$1\frac{1}{4}$–$1\frac{3}{4}$ kilo
Tokay or All Purpose yeast			
Water up to	1 gallon	1 gallon	5 litre

Peel and slice marrow, pour 3 pints boiling water over it, stir in 1 lb sugar, add equal quantity of cold water and the rest of the ingredients but keep back the remainder of the sugar. If it is intended to make a dry wine use an All Purpose yeast, if a sweet wine a Tokay yeast. Keep in a warm airing cupboard for two or three days, stirring twice daily. Strain and add the rest of the sugar dissolved in water, i.e. 1½ lb for a dry wine and 2½ lb for a sweet wine. Make up to 1 gallon and ferment on.

Mead

This is a wine made from honey diluted with water to produce dry or sweet table wines. Honeys vary considerably in flavour and for making dry mead it is preferable to use a bland pale honey such as that imported from New Zealand. As honey contains about 24 per cent water it is desirable to use from 3–3½ lb of honey for a dry mead and 5 lb for a sweet mead. The usual additions such as acid, tannin and Campden tablets are made and if the fermentation is a little sluggish the addition of Energizer will increase the fermentation rate. When making sweet mead a darker honey with a stronger taste can be used and particularly when making spiced mead. Spiced meads are called Metheglin if dry or Sack Metheglin if sweet. Pyment is made from grape juice sweetened with honey and Hippocras is spiced Pyment.

The spices used are the same as are used in cake making: cloves, mace, nutmeg, cinnamon, ginger and rosemary, which is particularly useful. Vermouth powder can also be used to produce very attractive spiced meads or aperitives.

Honey can also be used for producing Ale-like beverages.

Mead—Honey Ale

	BRITISH	U.S.A.	METRIC
Honey	1 lb 5 oz	1 lb	⅔ kilo
Yeast Nutrient	½ teasp.	½ teasp.	½ teasp.
Campden table	1	1	1
Hops	1 oz	¾ oz	30 gm.
Ale yeast			
Water up to	1 gallon	1 gallon	5 litre

Mead, dry

	BRITISH	U.S.A.	METRIC
Honey	3½ lb	3 lb	1¾ kilo
Yeast Nutrient	½ teasp.	½ teasp.	½ teasp.
Campden tablet	1	1	1
All Purpose yeast			
Water up to	1 gallon	1 gallon	5 litre

Mead, sweet (also called Sack Mead)

	BRITISH	U.S.A.	METRIC
Honey	5 lb	4 lb	2½ kilo
Yeast Nutrient	½ teasp.	½ teasp.	½ teasp.
Campden tablet	1	1	1
Madeira yeast			
Water up to	1 gallon	1 gallon	5 litre

Medlar Wine

	BRITISH	U.S.A.	METRIC
Medlars	8 lb	6 lb	4 kilo
Pectozyme	1 tablesp.	1 tablesp.	1 tablesp.
Yeast Nutrient	½ teasp.	½ teasp.	½ teasp.
Grape tannin	¼ teasp.	¼ teasp.	¼ teasp.
Campden tablets	2	2	2
Sugar	3 lb	2¾ lb	1½ kilo
Tokay or Sherry yeast			
Water up to	1 gallon	1 gallon	5 litre

(Method as for Greengage Wine)

Melon Wine (as Marrow Wine)

Metheglin (Dry Mead spiced) (see Mead)

Mulberry Wine*—Sherry-type

	BRITISH	U.S.A.	METRIC
Mulberries	5 lb	4 lb	2½ kilo
Yeast Nutrient	½ teasp.	½ teasp.	½ teasp.
Sugar	1 lb	¾ lb	½ kilo
Boiling water	6 pints	6 pints	4 litre
Cool and add Sherry yeast			

Ferment for three days then strain, press and add 2 pints of syrup prepared from 2 lb sugar and 1 pint boiling water.

Recipe by courtesy of Mr P. Upton, Salisbury, Southern Rhodesia.

* As mulberries easily go vinegar sour a Campden tablet could be used with advantage.

111

Mulberry Wine—Port-type (1 gallon)*
>5 lb Mulberries
>1 gallon water
>2 lb 14 oz–3 lb sugar
>½ teaspoon Yeast Nutrient
>2½ teaspoons citric acid
>¼ teaspoon Grape tannin
>Port Wine yeast or All Purpose wine yeast.

Do not stalk the fruit, just boil and add ingredients. Add wine yeast. Racking to take place as soon as fermentation ceases—twenty-one days. This will make an excellent before or after dinner heavy port. Bottle, adding ¾ oz of syrup to each bottle. Cork tightly, ready for drinking in eighteen months.

Recipe by courtesy of Mr T. Ward, Salisbury, Southern Rhodesia.

Author's note: Generally in this country it is wise to consume the wine soon after adding syrup but where the fermentation and maturing have been carried out in a warmer climate the wine may be stable enough for sweetening.

Nectarine Wine (as Apricot Wine)

Nettle Wine (as Blackberry Shoot Wine)
>2 quarts of nettles to the gallon.

Oak Leaf Wine Sweet

	BRITISH	U.S.A.	METRIC
Oak leaves	1 gallon	1 gallon	5 litre
Orange juice	10 oz	8 oz	300 ml
Lemon juice	6 oz	4½ oz	180 ml
Sugar	4 lb	3 lb	2 kilo
Campden tablets—	1	1	1
for sweet wine but not for Sherry			
Yeast Nutrient	1 teasp.	1 teasp.	1 teasp.
Sherry yeast or Madeira yeast			
Water up to	1 gallon	1 gallon	5 litre

Pour 4 pints boiling water over the leaves, stand for 24 hours, then strain. Warm the liquid to dissolve the sugar, add some more

* See footnote on previous page.

water to cool then add the juice of the oranges and lemons, nutrient and the yeast. Make up to 1 gallon and ferment on. Use less sugar for a dry wine.

Orange Wine (see Chapter 2)

Orange Wine (Canadian recipe)
>   3 Imperial gallons water
>   3 12 oz cans frozen orange juice
>   6 fresh oranges
>   10½ lb sugar
>   ½ oz Yeast Nutrient
>   3 lb chopped raisins
>   5 Campden tablets
>   All Purpose wine yeast

Dissolve frozen orange juice in hot water. Pour over sugar and stir thoroughly. Add sliced oranges and raisins and stir in Yeast Nutrient. Crush and dissolve Campden tablets, stir in. Cover and leave for 24 hours. Add previously prepared yeast, cover. Stir every other day for 14 days. Strain and put in gallon jugs.

Recipe by courtesy of Messrs Wine Art, Vancouver, B.C.

Pansy Wine (as Carnation)

Parsley Wine (see also page 57)

This is a really lovely wine mainly because there is little to ferment and the yeast has to work. As there is insufficient yeast food present some of the yeast will die and in doing so will confer flavour on the wine. Hence the importance of using a good yeast. For a dry wine use the All Purpose or Sauterne yeast; for a sweet wine the Tokay yeast is very valuable.

	BRITISH	U.S.A.	METRIC
Parsley	1 lb	¾ lb	½ kilo
Orange juice	12 oz	9 oz	400 ml
Lemon juice	4 oz	3 oz	120 ml
Yeast Nutrient	½ teasp.	½ teasp.	½ teasp.
Campden tablets	1	1	1
Sugar	2½–4 lb	2–3 lb	1¼–2 kilo
Water up to	1 gallon	1 gallon	5 litre

Wine yeast, either All Purpose, Sauterne or Tokay

Wine Recipes from A to Z

Pour boiling water over the parsley, leave overnight, strain, add the juice of oranges and lemons, Yeast Nutrient and sugar. Make up to 1 gallon. Fermentation will not be very fast but the wine will be lovely.

Parsnip Wine.

Most suitable as a sherry. Ferment as beetroot wine but using a Sherry yeast. Omit the Campden tablet.

Passion Fruit Wine

The fruit is also known as the Purple Grenadilla; it is somewhat like an elongated plum. Ferment as plum wine.

Pea Pod Wine

	BRITISH	U.S.A.	METRIC
Pea pods	4 lb	3 lb	2 kilo
Sugar	3½ lb	2¾ lb	1¾ kilo
Citric acid	1 tablesp.	1 tablesp.	1 tablesp.
Yeast Energizer	½ teasp.	½ teasp.	½ teasp.
Grape tannin	½ teasp.	½ teasp.	½ teasp.
Campden tablets	1	1	1
Tokay yeast			
Water to	1 gallon	1 gallon	5 litre

Boil the pea pods in half the amount of water till soft, then stir in the sugar. Leave till lukewarm then add the remaining ingredients and make up to 1 gallon.

Peach Wine (as Apricot Wine)

Peach Pulp Wine (as Apricot Pulp Wine)

Pear Wine

	BRITISH	U.S.A.	METRIC
Pears, minced	4 lb	3 lb	2 kilo
Citric acid	1 tablesp.	1 tablesp.	1 tablesp.
Sugar	2 lb	1½ lb	1 kilo
Yeast Energizer	½ teasp.	½ teasp.	½ teasp.
Campden tablets	2	2	2
Chablis yeast			
Water to	1 gallon	1 gallon	5 litre

The fruit is minced and at once mixed with 2 Campden tablets dissolved in a little water. The pulp is left 24 hours and then strained through a hessian cloth or bag. The juice is made up to 1 gallon with lukewarm water and the other ingredients are then added.

Perry

This beverage resembles cider in that it is produced from the milled or grated fruit without the addition of sugar. Pears are very high in tannin and by leaving the pulp for 24 hours before pressing some of the tannin will become insoluble and the juice will be less astringent. To prevent fermentation and darkening during this period, about four crushed Campden tablets are stirred into the pulp produced from 16 lb of pears. The following day the liquid strained from the pulp is transferred to a gallon jar, an All Purpose or Champagne yeast is added and one teaspoon of Yeast Nutrient. When the fermentation is over the Perry is left to clear and racked. It should be stored for 3 to 6 months and racked again. It can then be rendered brilliant by fining and bottled in pint screw-top bottles with one good teaspoon of sugar to each bottle. It is bound to produce some more yeast, but if the bottle is stood upright and chilled before pouring, provided that an All Purpose yeast has been used, most of the yeast will remain adhering to the bottom of the bottle.

Pineapple Wine

	BRITISH	U.S.A.	METRIC
Pineapples, chopped finely	3–4 lb	2¼–3 lb	1½–2 kilo
Sugar	3–4 lb	2¼–3 lb	1½–2 kilo
Campden tablets	1	1	1
Yeast Nutrient	½ teasp.	½ teasp.	½ teasp.
Grape tannin	¼ teasp.	¼ teasp.	¼ teasp.
Citric acid	1 tablesp.	1 tablesp.	1 tablesp.
All Purpose wine yeast			
Water up to	1 gallon	1 gallon	5 litre

The pineapple should be chopped and covered with hot water, Campden tablet, 1 lb of sugar, citric acid and Nutrient are added.

Enough water is then added to bring this mixture down to blood heat before adding the yeast. Ferment on the pulp for three days then press. Add the rest of the sugar, using the smaller quantity for a semi-sweet wine. Make up to 1 gallon and ferment on. A delicious liqueur-like wine can be produced by doubling the fruit content but citric acid must be omitted.

Plum Wine

Victoria plums, 3 to 4 lb per gallon, make a pleasant rosé table wine with an All Purpose yeast. Purple plums are excellent for wines which are to resemble Sherry and Madeira. For Sherry allow 4 lb of fruit to the gallon (see Rosehip Wine), and for a sweet Madeira 6 lb are not too much. Plums, like all stone fruits, are high in pectin so a pectic enzyme must be used.

Method. Proceed as for Greengage Wine or if Sherry is wanted as for Rosehip Wine.

Pomegranate Wine

This fruit is excessively high in tannin. The juice can be obtained by pressing the whole fruit in a press, but it must on no account be minced, as this will extract too much tannin. If the juice is treated with 3 Campden tablets and left overnight 1 to two pints of the juice can be used to produce a gallon of wine.

Port type

Port is produced commercially from red grapes which are pulped and partly fermented. The pulp is pressed and when the sugar content has dropped to around half, alcohol is added to stop the fermentation. Some concentrated grape juice is also added and several times during the period that the port remains in storage small quantities of alcohol are added. Ports, with the exception of vintage Ports, are blended prior to shipment, and this requires great knowledge and skill. A wine resembling Port can be made from elderberries or a blend of elderberries and grapes. Other fruits which are suitable for the making of similar sweet, strong, red wines are bilberry, blackberry, damson, loganberry and wineberry. To obtain Port character a Port yeast must be used and the fruit content should be as high as possible; sugar must be added in stages. (See Elderberry Wine Port type.)

Primrose Wine (as Broom Wine)

Prune Wine (as Plum Wine)

Prune Wine, dried (as Currant Wine)

Pyment (see Mead)

Quince Wine

	BRITISH	U.S.A.	METRIC
Quinces, pulped	4 lb	3 lb	2 kilo
Campden tablets	2	2	2
Yeast Nutrient	½ teasp.	½ teasp.	½ teasp.
Pectozyme	1 tablesp.	1 tablesp.	1 tablesp.
Citric acid	½ tablesp.	½ tablesp.	½ tablesp.
Sugar	3–4 lb	2¼–3 lb	1½–2 kilo
All Purpose wine yeast			
Water up to	1 gallon	1 gallon	5 litre

Ferment with 1 lb of sugar on pulp which has been covered with warm, not boiling, water in which the Campden tablets have been dissolved. Add all the other ingredients and after three to five days strain. Dissolve the rest of the sugar in some hot water, add, make up to 1 gallon and ferment on. If desired 1 lb of minced sultanas can be added to the quinces prior to fermenting on the pulp. The fruit from the Ornamental quince is said to be suitable for winemaking; it needs to be boiled to soften it and is frequently extremely acid.

Raisin Wine (as Currant Wine)

Raspberry Wine (as Blackberry Wine, but without added acid)

Redcurrant Wine Dry

	BRITISH	U.S.A.	METRIC
Redcurrants	2 lb	1½ lb	1 kilo
Blackcurrants	1 lb	¾ lb	½ kilo
or Dried elderberries	¼ lb	¼ lb	125 gm
Sugar	2¼ lb	1¾ lb	1⅛ kilo
Pectozyme	1 tablesp.	1 tablesp.	1 tablesp.
Yeast Nutrient	½ teasp.	½ teasp.	½ teasp.
Campden tablets	1	1	1
All Purpose wine yeast			
Water up to	1 gallon	1 gallon	5 litre

Method as for Blackcurrant.

Rhubarb Wine

The author has developed a much improved method for making Rhubarb wine. This consists in covering the rhubarb with dry sugar until this has gone to juice, straining off the juice and washing out the sugar which has remained entrained in the pulp with cold water. By this method the acid content is kept low, the juice is not harsh and is practically free from pectin. This method has also been tried with fresh peaches and has proved successful. The rhubarb should be used in May and not peeled. Three pounds of rhubarb are sliced thinly or chopped, and 3 lb of dry sugar added. Cover fruit with the sugar and leave for twenty-four hours or more until most of the sugar has dissolved, strain off. Stir pulp in some water and strain again. Make up to 1 gallon, add a wine yeast and a teaspoon of Yeast Nutrient. If the wine is to taste of rhubarb omit Campden tablets but if a wine like a Hock is wanted add 2 Campden tablets and ferment on.

Rice Wine

	BRITISH	U.S.A.	METRIC
Patna polished rice	3 lb	2¼ lb	1½ kilo
Boiling water to cover			
Sultanas, minced	½ lb	½ lb	¼ kilo
Yeast Energizer	½ teasp.	½ teasp.	½ teasp.
Citric acid	2 tablesp.	2 tablesp.	2 tablesp.
Grape tannin	1 teasp.	1 teasp.	1 teasp.
Campden tablets	1	1	1
Sugar	3½–4 lb	2½–3 lb	1¾–2 kilo

Cereal wine yeast together with Tokay yeast

Water up to	1 gallon	1 gallon	5 litre

Leave the rice and sultanas covered over in a warm place overnight then add the other ingredients. Strain, make up to 1 gallon and ferment on.

Rosehip Wine

This fruit makes a very nice Sherry-type wine.

	BRITISH	U.S.A.	METRIC
Rosehips, crushed	4 lb	3 lb	2 kilo
Orange juice	10 oz	8 oz	300 ml
Pectozyme	1 tablesp.	1 tablesp.	1 tablesp.
Citric acid	½ tablesp.	½ tablesp.	½ tablesp.
Sugar	2–3 lb	1½–2¼ lb	1–1½ kilo
Yeast Energizer	1 teasp.	1 teasp.	1 teasp.
Sherry yeast			
Water up to	6 pint	6 pint	4 litre

Pour boiling water over fruit, add one pound of sugar and acid. When cool enough add orange juice, Pectozyme, Energizer and the yeast. Leave in a warm cupboard 3 to 5 days then strain off and add the remaining sugar making up to *6 pints only*. Ferment in container which is only ¾ full and lightly plugged with cotton wool. The extra air will help to give a Sherry character.

Rosepetal Wine, Dry

Red rose petals make a wonderful wine, especially with a Chablis yeast (see also page 42).

	BRITISH	U.S.A.	METRIC
Rose petals	1 gallon	1 gallon	5 litre
Boiling water	1 gallon	1 gallon	5 litre
Sugar	2½ lb	2 lb	1¼ kilo
The juice of 2 lemons			
Yeast Nutrient	½ teasp.	½ teasp.	½ teasp.
Campden tablets	1	1	1
Chablis yeast			

Pour the water over the petals and allow to stand for twenty-four hours. Strain, squeeze well, dissolve the sugar with a little warming, add the lemon juice, Nutrient and a Chablis yeast.

Rosemary Wine

Although the young shoots can be treated like blackberry shoots, the scent of the rosemary is so strong that a very pleasant wine can be made by soaking some bruised shoots in a neutral wine such as an apple or pear wine. This makes a good aperitif.

Rowanberry Wine (as Hawthornberry Wine)

Sauterne-type Wine

The luscious wines of the Sauterne and Barsac region of France are made from berries which have been disintegrated by the 'Noble Pourriture' or 'Noble Mould'. The mould feeds on the juice, increases the sugar content and reduces the acid content. The yeast, which is also present on the skins, now has a hard task to ferment a juice high in sugar and lacking in nutrients. The gravities of these juices can be extremely high and the fermentation is often sluggish and prolonged through several periods of sticking. Prior to fermentation, that is as soon as the mouldy grapes have been pressed, massive doses of sulphite amounting to 9 Campden tablets per gallon are added. The flavour of the wine is influenced by this high sulphite content, but far more so by fermenting in a warm climate, but under adverse food conditions for the yeast. This leads to yeast autolysis which with the right yeast produces Sauterne flavours. It is possible to make from Apricots for instance a wine identical to a Sauterne by keeping the fruit content very low, fermenting warm and adding from 4 to $4\frac{1}{2}$ lb of sugar right at the start of fermentation.

Sherry-type Wine

Sherries are essentially different from table wines. In all wine-making the greatest care is taken to prevent air affecting the wine. This is done by including Campden tablets in the recipe, by keeping containers bung full, by using an airlock containing water to prevent access of air and by adding Reductone tablets to the finished wine.

In Sherry production the juice is agitated by treading, thus incorporating a lot of air and the fermentation is violent; as soon as this is over and the lees have settled the wine is drawn off and transferred to another container with renewed aeration. The new container is kept only $\frac{7}{8}$ full, and the wine is not racked again but left on the renewed sediment and exposed to air. To prevent off flavours the wine is fortified to about 17 per cent alcohol. It is blended through an ingenious system called a solera which is fully discussed in *Amateur Wine Making*. To achieve similar character in a wine is not difficult but does require considerable time as the Sherry flavour only becomes pronounced with ageing. Fruits suitable for producing Sherry-type wines are orange, blackberry, gooseberry, apple, rosehip, strawberry and plum (but not damson, Victoria or greengage).

Sloe Wine

	BRITISH	U.S.A.	METRIC
Sloes	2 lb	1½ lb	1 kilo
Pectozyme	1 tablesp.	1 tablesp.	1 tablesp.
Yeast Energizer	½ teasp.	½ teasp.	½ teasp.
Campden tablet	1	1	1
Sugar	3 lb	2¼ lb	1½ kilo
All Purpose wine yeast			
Water up to	1 gallon	1 gallon	5 litre

Method as for Greengage Wine. The sloes must be very or over-ripe to decrease both the acid and the tannin content.

Strawberry Wine

	BRITISH	U.S.A.	METRIC
Strawberries	5 lb	4 lb	2½ kilo
Sugar	3 lb	2¼ lb	1½ kilo
Campden tablets	2	2	2

These are omitted if a Sherry yeast is used.

Wash strawberries, mash and cover with sugar. Leave for twenty-four hours then strain off the syrup and add some water to the pulp and strain again. Make up to 1 gallon.

Next add:

	BRITISH	U.S.A.	METRIC
Citric acid	2 tablesp.	2 tablesp.	2 tablesp.
Yeast Energizer	½ teasp.	½ teasp.	½ teasp.
Grape tannin	½ teasp.	½ teasp.	½ teasp.
All Purpose or Sherry yeast			
Water up to	1 gallon	1 gallon	5 litre

Ferment on.

Wine Recipes from A to Z

Sultana Wine (as Currant Wine)

Squash Wine (as Marrow Wine)

Tangerine Wine (as Orange Wine)

Tea Wine

This is really a dried fruit wine in which use is made of strong tea to give astringency instead of grape tannin.

Tomato Wine

	BRITISH	U.S.A.	METRIC
Tomatoes, fully ripe	5 lb	3¾ lb	2½ kilo
Pectozyme	1 tablesp.	1 tablesp.	1 tablesp.
Yeast Nutrient	½ teasp.	½ teasp.	½ teasp.
Citric acid	1½ tablesp.	1½ tablesp.	1½ tablesp.
Sugar	2½ lb	2 lb	1¼ kilo
Campden tablets	1	1	1
All Purpose wine yeast			
Water up to	1 gallon	1 gallon	5 litre

Boil tomatoes in 3 pints of water. Mash, add equal quantity of cold water and the rest of the ingredients. Leave overnight, then strain off and ferment on.

Vine Prunings

	BRITISH	U.S.A.	METRIC
Vine leaves or unripe berries	4 pints	4 pints	2½ litre
Boiling water	4 pints	4 pints	2½ litre
Sugar	2½ lb	2 lb	1¼ kilo
Orange juice	10 oz	8 oz	300 ml
Yeast Energizer	1 teasp.	1 teasp.	1 teasp.
Campden tablets	1	1	1
All Purpose wine yeast			
Water up to	1 gallon	1 gallon	5 litre

Wallflower Wine (as Elderflower Wine)

Walnut Leaf Wine (as Oak Leaf Wine)

Wine Recipes from A to Z

Wheat Wine (as Maize Wine)

Whin Wine (as Gorse Wine)

Whitecurrant Wine

	BRITISH	U.S.A.	METRIC
Ripe whitecurrants	2 lb	1½ lb	1 kilo
Boiling water	2 pints	2 pints	1¼ litre
Mash, and add sugar	2 lb	1½ lb	1 kilo
Cold water	2 pints	2 pints	1¼ litre
Pectozyme	1 tablesp.	1 tablesp.	1 tablesp.
Yeast Nutrient	½ teasp.	½ teasp.	½ teasp.
Campden tablets	1	1	1
All Purpose wine yeast			
Water up to	1 gallon	1 gallon	5 litre

Leave in a warm place overnight then strain and make up to 1 gallon.

Whortleberry Wine (another name for Bilberry)

Wineberry Wine (as Blackberry Wine)

Yarrow Wine (as Burnet Wine)

Zinnia Wine

This flower has not been tried out by the author for winemaking but it should be possible to use the florets just as daisies are used for winemaking. Anyhow, there was no other fruit or ingredient which started with the letter Z!!

13

Wine Faults—their Prevention and Cure

It is very unusual these days to find that wines produced by amateurs are diseased. They may have faults, such as lack of clarity or bad flavours, but the care that is lavished by winemakers on their hobby bears its own reward. It is, of course, much easier to look after wines which are made in small quantities. In bulk production there is much greater danger of disease and in commercial winemaking the use of sulphite has always been resorted to. Without this, sound wines could not be produced and much wine would become *vinegar sour*. It is most important to guard against this disease and this is done by the use of sound fruit, by protection from air by the addition of Campden tablets, and by keeping the containers bung full. Vinegar bacteria are often present on damaged fruit and even slight traces of vinegar will stop the fermentation and give a wine which is low in alcohol. When exposed to air the alcohol can turn into vinegar, but once the alcohol content is above 10 per cent the wine is unlikely to become vinegar sour.

The next disease to guard against is *oiliness*. *Torula* and other bacteria are able to produce a mucilage which renders the wine thick and ropy. *Torula* are sometimes found in dry yeast. Such wine will pour like a thick oil but it can be rendered drinkable by breaking down the mucilage through intense agitation or beating with a whisk. The wine will now have the normal fluid consistency

124

and should be sulphited with 2 Campden tablets to the gallon. I personally would not wish to drink such a wine, and would sooner pour it away.

The third is a disease called *Flowers of Wine*. This is caused through a yeast-like organism called *Mycoderma* found on fruit together with wild yeast and bacteria. The use of sulphite prevents mycodermi from developing. The Flowers of Wine at first form a thin silky white skin which tends to creep up on the sides of the vessel. Later this skin becomes thick and wrinkled but tends to break up very easily. Wine which develops this disease must be given at least 2 Campden tablets to the gallon and kept in containers which are bung full. The best way to remove these Flowers of Wine is to fill the container to overflowing which will cause the skin to flow off first. Flowers of wine do not develop if the alcohol content of the wine is above 10%. When topping up the fermenter with water it is important to stir the wine so that the top layer has the same alcohol content as the rest of the wine.

Haziness is mainly due to unsuitable preparation of the must. Nine times out of ten hazy wines are those in which the pectin has not broken down. To find out whether the haze is due to pectin, test by mixing a tablespoon of the wine with 2 tablespoons of methylated spirit. If this results in an intensification of the haze and the settling out of a white clot of jelly, then pectin was the cause. Do not forget to throw away this treated portion. Pectin can be removed by the addition of 1 tablespoon of Pectozyme to the gallon, then leaving the wine in a warm airing cupboard for a few days and following up by fining the wine. Other hazes can be due to metallic contamination both by copper or by iron; citric acid will remove these hazes. A metallic taste can be removed by stirring 2 ozs of bran into the gallon of wine, leaving for a few days and filtering.

Bitterness. This can occur in wines made from red fruits and is mainly due to decomposition of the red pigments by mould. The only remedy is to avoid the use of mouldy red fruit. Mouldy white grapes do not cause the same problem.

Darkening is frequently due to lack of or delayed addition of sulphite and should not occur if a good technique is employed.

Off Flavours. These are mainly due to unsatisfactory fermentation such as fermenting juices in the presence of insufficient acid.

Wine Faults—their Prevention and Cure

Bacteria may also produce flavours resembling bad butter or pickled cabbage or even a medicinal tang, while some wild yeasts produce an odour of pear drops.

All these faults can be avoided by the proper adjustment of the juice with acid, the use of Campden tablets to suppress undesirable bacteria and wild yeasts, and the addition of a wine yeast starter in a vigorously fermenting condition.

14

Home Brewing of Beer—
Beer Recipes

Prior to April 1963 home brewing without a licence was not permitted, though no official notice appears to have been taken of the small amount of brewing undertaken by amateurs. Now home brewing is brought into line with domestic winemaking and, provided the beer is not sold, the amateur can brew as much as he likes.

Brewing, like winemaking, is a fermentation process depending on the action of yeast. As it is not the case with wines, the production of beer takes a matter of weeks rather than months and the beer needs little time for maturing. The alcohol content should be less than that of wines and ranges from $3\frac{1}{2}$ per cent to 7 per cent. The latter would be more in the nature of a Barley Wine.

Beer is an effervescent beverage and can be made to retain its effervescence, but most commercial beers are carbonated just as soda-water is. A dry beer after maturing for a few weeks followed by racking and fining, will remain reasonably clear and no further yeast will grow. The head in the beer is supplied by the carbon dioxide gas being forced into the beer under pressure. The gas is released on removing the stopper and pouring the beer. Home carbonators are available but of course expensive, though worth while for beer addicts.

The beer is rendered sparkling by a method similar to that used for Champagne; about $\frac{1}{2}$ to 1 oz of sugar is added to each gallon of beer which is at once bottled and then will start a second fermentation in the bottle. This addition is called *priming* and the effect is to render the beer sparkling. This is called conditioning the beer. Those liking a beer with a fair head are advised to use 1 oz of sugar to the gallon. It is also a help to use a heading liquid as this helps to retain the foam. After a while a new yeast deposit will form and the beer will become charged with carbon dioxide gas just as happens in making Champagne. The yeast deposit can either be retained in the bottle or removed prior to consumption. An excellent way of doing this is to bottle the beer in Champagne bottles and to use hollow plastic stoppers. A day or so before it is wanted, wrap the bottle in a towel, shake well to dislodge the deposit and stand the beer upside down in the refrigerator. Most of the yeast will collect in the plastic cork. Loosen the cork by holding the bottle neck under water and as the cork comes away bring the bottle, which should now be free from the deposit, upright and pour out the beer, or re-insert a clean cork and store the beer for future use.

Having now shown how to carbonate the beer let us consider how it is made and in what way it differs from wine. Wines are made mostly from fruit juices and vegetables, though flowers and cereals can also be used. Beer on the other hand is produced from cereals which have undergone a process known as malting. The cereals, mainly barley and to a smaller extent wheat, are sprouted. This brings about changes in the grain and produces an enzyme called diastase. At the right temperature this enzyme has the power of converting starch to malt sugar, and this is the process carried out in commercial beer brewing. The solution of malt obtained from the grain can be filtered and concentrated to produce a malt extract. Concentrating this extract under carefully controlled temperature conditions makes the malt extract expensive. Therefore to use it on a large scale would be uneconomic, but it is ideal for the home producer whose beer can then be very close to commercial beer in quality. Those wishing to do their own malting are referred to *Amateur Wine Making*, where this is fully described. It is simpler and just as cheap to brew beer in the home either from bought malted barley or malt extract.

Home brewing depends much more on the skill and experience of the brewer than winemaking does. Beer making differs from winemaking in that no definite intervals of racking can be laid down, and beer quality is much influenced by fermenting conditions, the hardness and other mineral content of the water, and by the temperatures prevailing during the brewing and the conditioning of the beer in the bottle.

It is evident that good beer can be produced from malt extract with, if desired, added grains and sugar, and of course the use of a suitable yeast. As beer making is fairly straightforward we will cover the production of different types of beer under the heading of *Beer recipes*, but the general rules which should be adhered to are:

A. Keep the sugar and malt content low enough to give a beer at the right alcohol level as outlined in Table V. Small quantities of cereals added, from 4 to 8 oz per gallon, do not affect the alcohol content significantly but do give a beer with more body and better foaming quality.

B. Adjust the hop content to the type of beer that is being made, as in Table V, page 130.

C. Be sure to boil the malt extract or malted grain together with some of the hops, as this boiling helps to give a beer which clears well. Just to dissolve the malt in hot water and then add the hops which have been boiled in water is insufficient. The two must be boiled together. Some of the hop flavour will be lost during the boil so it is as well to keep a quarter of the hops back and only add these to the hot brew just prior to cooling. It may not be convenient to boil the malt and the hops in the full amount of water needed for the brew but less can be used. Extra water can then be added afterwards but in districts where water on boiling tends to scum, all the water should be boiled before use.

D. Half a Campden tablet added to each gallon at the first racking frequently improves the beer.

E. A sedimentary Lager Beer yeast will make for early clarification and will make the pouring of the beer conditioned in the bottle more satisfactory.

F. Ferment warm in a wide-mouthed container which allows for stirring and as soon as the fermentation slows down stir well and transfer with the yeast deposit to suitable jars fitted with an air-lock. Complete fermentation in a cool place. Then rack, prime with extra sugar* and bottle. It is of course

* See Light Lager Beer recipe.

possible to bottle the beer while it still contains some un-fermented sugar which will give a head after 2 to 3 weeks. This is done by testing the beer with a Clinitest (obtainable from a Pharmacist at 10/–). When the sugar content is between $\frac{3}{4}$ per cent and $\frac{1}{2}$ per cent the beer must be bottled promptly.

Once having made a satisfactory home brew, it is highly desir-able to stick to the same fermenting and conditioning tempera-tures and the same proportion of ingredients. No hard-and-fast rules can be laid down for home brewers, but the following recipes present a good selection of the various types of beer that can be produced.

Finally, if on opening beer which has been primed or bottled with some residual sugar the pressure of the gas seems excessive, allow some to escape for a while, then screw down again and allow the beer to settle by leaving in a cold place for a few days.

TABLE V

Additions of Sugar and Hops for Beer Production

Type of Beer	Starting Gravity	Approx. Alcohol content by volume	Malt Extract per gallon	Sugar	Hops
Lager	30	3.7%	$\frac{1}{2}$ lb	6 oz	$\frac{1}{2}$ oz
Pale Ale	35	4.4%	$\frac{1}{2}$ lb	$\frac{1}{2}$ lb	$\frac{1}{2}$ oz
Ale or Stout	45	5.8%	$\frac{1}{2}$ lb	$\frac{3}{4}$ lb	$\frac{3}{4}$ oz
Strong Ale	60	7.8%	1 lb	$\frac{3}{4}$ lb	$\frac{3}{4}$ oz
Barley Wine					
either	80	10%	1 lb	$\frac{1}{2}$ lb	2 oz
or	80	10%	2 lb	$\frac{1}{4}$ lb	2 oz

Please note that the Malt Extract referred to in this table is a thick Malt Extract and not a liquid Malt Extract.

The making of Beer has been discussed in general terms in the preceding pages and the ingredients which are used to produce different types of beer are given in Table V. For those who do not wish to compile their own recipes a number of these are included. The recipes will be for 2 gallons and for U.S.A. measures the quantities of malt and sugar and hops used per two U.S.A. gallons will be approximately $\frac{3}{4}$ of the British measure, while Metric equivalents are roughly ½ kilo to correspond to 1 lb and 10 litres to correspond with 2 gallons. The procedure outlined for the first recipe can be followed in each case as the beer recipes will be those produced from malt extract and sugar with some blended malt to give body, head retention and colour.

Light Lager Beer

> 2 gallon water
> 1 lb malt extract
> ¾ lb sugar
> 1 oz hops
> 2 oz pale blended malt
> 2 teaspoon salt
> 1½ teaspoon citric acid
> 2 teaspoon Yeast Energizer
> 1 liquid Beer yeast
> 1 Campden tablet

Transfer the malt extract and most of the hops to no less than 4 pints of hot water, bring to the boil and keep boiling for half an hour. Add the rest of the hops, blended malts, sugar, salt and citric acid. Stir to dissolve. Allow to cool and strain off. Make up to 2 gallons with tepid water, add the Yeast Energizer and beer yeast and leave in a warm cupboard until foaming almost ceases. Stir well, transfer to a 2-gallon jar, or two 1-gallon jars, insert air-lock and leave in a cool place until the yeast has settled and the beer has cleared. Now the beer is racked off into a pail and if the gravity is below 1 then the beer is primed with 2 oz of cane sugar dissolved in some water which is stirred into the beer. This is followed by 1 teaspoon of gelatin first softened in cold water and then dissolved by the addition of boiling water. But if the gravity is above 5 then 1 oz of cane sugar is sufficient. Stir in one crushed Campden tablet and then transfer the beer to proper beer bottles, stopper and leave standing upright. After 2 or 3 weeks at room temperature the beer should be sparkling and the yeast deposit in the bottom of the bottle should be firm enough to allow most of the beer to be poured off easily.

If it is desired to have a beer free from a yeast deposit then use Champagne or other strong bottles fitted with a hollow plastic cork, and leave the bottles lying on their sides. When a good yeast

131

deposit has been noted bring the deposit down into the cork by standing the bottles cork down. It will take a week or so and require slight twisting jerks to disengage the yeast. For safety's sake it is as well to wrap the bottle in a towel while shaking down the yeast. Chill well in a refrigerator. Remove the plastic cork by holding the bottle neck downwards in a basin of water and as soon as the cork is out bring the bottle to the pouring position.

N.B. It is always desirable to chill beer before consumption.

For those who require a beer with more head the amount of sugar to the gallon can be increased to 2–4 oz to 2 gallon, but only if the gravity of the beer before the sugar addition is below one. As many beer drinkers appreciate a lasting foam a heading liquid added to the beer at the rate of ½ oz to the gallon will cause improved head retention.

Ale or Stout

2 gallon water
1 lb malt extract
1½ lb sugar
1½ oz hops
8 oz pale blended malt (or chocolate malt for Stout)
2 teaspoon Plaster of Paris
1½ teaspoon citric acid
2 teaspoon salt
2 teaspoon Yeast Energizer
1 liquid Beer yeast
1 Campden tablet

Method as for Lager Beer but add the Plaster of Paris to the 2 gallons of water, all of which must be boiled before use.

Strong Ale

2 gallon water
2 lb malt extract
1½ lb sugar
1½–2 oz of hops
2 teaspoon Plaster of Paris
2 teaspoon salt
1½ teaspoon citric acid
2 teaspoon Yeast Energizer

              1 liquid Beer yeast

              1 Campden tablet

Method as before.

Milk Stout

              2 gallon water

              1 lb black patent malt

              4 oz flaked barley

              1 oz hops

              1 lb sugar

              2 teaspoon citric acid

              4 oz lactose or milk sugar

              Stout yeast

Pour hot but not boiling water over the patent malt and stir in the flaked barley. Leave covered for twenty-four hours, strain. Boil the hops in 2 pints of water, strain. Dissolve sugar and lactose in the hot liquid and add to bulk. Follow by the yeast and ferment to completion. Allow to clear. Rack carefully into pint bottles which contain ½ teaspoonful sugar. Leave three weeks before drinking.

Oatmeal Stout

              2 gallon water

              1 lb roasted malt

              1 lb crystal malt

              2 lb Barbados sugar

              8 oz flaked maize

              2 teaspoons citric acid

              1–2 oz of hops

              Stout yeast

Pour hot, but not boiling, water over the malt, stir in the flaked maize, cover and leave overnight. Strain. Boil the hops in some of the water, strain, stir in sugar and citric acid and Stout yeast. Make up to 2 gallon. Ferment to completion, allow to clear, draw off carefully into pint pottles containing ½–1 teaspoonful of sugar. (It is best to put sugar into the bottles rather than into the beer as putting the sugar last will cause the beer to foam and lose a lot of its condition.)

Birch Sap Beer

This can be made from the sap obtained from the Silver Birch (see Birch Sap Wine p. 87). It will be very much like the continental white beer and is ideal as a shandy when mixed just prior to consumption with lemonade or raspberry syrup.

>1 gallon birch sap
>1 lb white sugar
>Juice of 2 lemons
>1 liquid Ale yeast

A little lemon peel improves the flavour of this beer.

Botanic Beer—Herb Beer

>2 oz dried meadowsweet ⎫
>2 oz dried betony   ⎪ or a packet of
>2 oz dried agrimony   ⎰ Botanic Beer
>2 oz dried raspberry leaves ⎭
>2 lb sugar
>½ lb malt extract
>1 teaspoon citric acid
>1 teaspoon Yeast Energizer

Pour 1 gallon boiling water over all the ingredients, cool to blood heat and add Ale yeast.

Bran Ale

>1 lb bran
>2 oz hops
>2 lb Demerara sugar
>1 lb malt extract
>Gravy browning if desired
>Ale or Lager Beer yeast
>Water up to 2 gallon

Burdock Ale

>1 oz burdock root
>½ oz chamomile heads
>¾ oz ginger
>1 lb sugar

1 lb malt extract
1 teaspoon citric acid
1 teaspoon Yeast Energizer
Ale yeast
Water up to 2 gallon

Boil the burdock root for 15 minutes in water, then proceed as for Botanic Beer.

Chamomile Beer

2 oz chamomile flower
$\frac{1}{2}$ oz ground ginger
$\frac{1}{2}$ lb malt extract
2 lb sugar
1 teaspoon citric acid
1 teaspoon Yeast Energizer
Ale yeast
Water up to 2 gallon

Method as for Botanic Beer

Dandelion Beer

$\frac{1}{2}$ lb young dandelion plants with tap root
1 lb Demerara sugar
$\frac{1}{2}$ oz crushed root ginger
Juice of 2 lemons
Liquid Ale yeast
Water to 1 gallon

Boil the washed roots in some of the water, cool and add the rest of the ingredients. Ferment until most of the sugar has gone, then bottle.

Ginger Beer

1 oz root ginger, crushed
$\frac{1}{2}$ oz cream of tartar
$\frac{1}{4}$ oz citric acid
1 lb white sugar
$\frac{1}{2}$ teaspoon Yeast Energizer
Liquid Ale yeast
Water to 1 gallon

Nettle Beer

As Dandelion Beer, but use 1 gallon of young nettles, bring to the boil with water, cool and strain.

Spruce Beer

> 1 lb treacle or 1 lb malt extract
> 2 lb sugar
> 2 tablespoon Essence of Spruce
> Ale yeast
> Water to 2 gallon

15

Aperitives and Liqueurs

Aperitives

Aperitives can be of two kinds—dry Sherries and White Ports or else spiced and fortified wines such as Dubonnet, Campari, Cinzano, French and Italian Vermouth.

Generally the alcohol content of aperitives ranges from 18 per cent to 22 per cent. As a wine by normal fermentation does not generally attain an alcoholic content above 15 per cent, more alcohol has to be added; frequently also extra sugar is required. The sugar content can vary considerably; dry Vermouth contains about 4 per cent and sweet Vermouth about 18 per cent.

Dry Vermouth

Sweet, home-produced wines such as apple, pear or gooseberry may contain anything from 5 to 10 per cent of sugar. The best way to ascertain whether this wine is of suitable sweetness is to compare it with a commercial French Vermouth. It is blended with a sweeter or drier wine until it is a little sweeter than the dry Vermouth that is to be matched. To 24 oz of the wine are added 2 oz of 140° proof Vodka. Into this is suspended a butter-muslin bag containing a teaspoonful of French Vermouth herbs and after a few days the Vermouth is tasted. If not sufficiently flavoured the bag is squeezed or, if necessary, kept suspended a little longer.

Aperitives and Liqueurs

French Vermouth

	BRITISH	U.S.A.	METRIC
Semi-sweet white wine	24 oz	24 oz	1 litre
Vodka 140° proof	2 oz	2 oz	80 ml
French Vermouth herbs	1 teasp.	1 teasp.	2 teasp.

The herbs are soaked in fortified wine for a few days. It is then adjusted with acids and tannin as required.

Sweet Vermouth

A normal sweet wine with an alcohol content of 14 per cent to 15 per cent will not be sweet enough so more sugar has to be added. Suppose wine with 14 per cent alcohol and 10 per cent sugar is to be converted to an aperitif with 20 per cent alcohol and 18 per cent sugar. As sugar addition increases the volume of the base wine by about 6/10 the weight of the sugar it will also, through the increase in volume, reduce the sugar and alcohol content of the base wine. As only a few are likely to wish to delve into the complex calculations which this involves, the recipe below will be found suitable for most purposes. The addition of Vermouth herbs is carried out as in French Vermouth but Italian Vermouth herbs must be used. Tannin and extra citric acid may also be needed and the aperitif may need filtering or fining.

Italian Vermouth

	BRITISH	U.S.A.	METRIC
Sugar	3 oz	2¼ oz	150 gm
Sweet White Wine	1 pint	1 pint	1 litre
Vodka 140° proof	3 oz	2¼ oz	150 mil
Italian Vermouth herbs	1 teasp.	1 teasp.	2 teasp.

Tannin and citric acid as required.

Egg Flip

Egg Flip is sometimes taken as an aperitif and at other times consumed as a liqueur, and can be really delicious. As it contains as much as 20 per cent of sugar and 18 per cent of alcohol, both extra sugar and extra alcohol have to be added to the base wine. The recipe given below has proved extremely successful.

	BRITISH	U.S.A.	METRIC
Egg yolks	4	4	4
Egg white	$\frac{1}{2}$	$\frac{1}{2}$	$\frac{1}{2}$
Sweet wine	20 oz	20 oz	500 ml
Castor sugar	3 oz	3 oz	75 gm
Vodka 140° proof	3 oz	3 oz	75 ml

The egg yolks and whites are lightly beaten until uniform and transferred to a double saucepan, the lower half of which is filled with hot water. One pint of a sweet white wine mixed with 3 oz of sugar and 3 oz of Vodka is added to the egg yolks with stirring. The temperature is allowed to rise slowly but not above 100° F. The mixture must be kept stirred and then it will thicken. It is then to be removed from the heat, a drop or two of Vanilla Essence are added, and the mixture is ready for bottling. If it has curdled, putting the mixture through a domestic cream-making machine will disperse the curd and produce a smooth product.

Liqueurs

The alcohol content of liqueurs varies considerably. Generally the fruit liqueurs like Cherry Brandy and Apricot Brandy are lower in alcohol strength than liqueurs which contain oils, like Crème de Menthe, or orange-flavoured liqueurs like Cointreau and Curaçao; while those which are flavoured with spices like Chartreuse and Bénédictine are even more alcoholic. There are several methods the amateur can use for making liqueurs. One of these is to soak the fruit in alcohol or brandy; the other is to use a wine as a base, fortify with extra alcohol, sweeten it, and add liqueur flavours.* The former method is much more expensive and only one example of it will be given here.

Sloe Gin

Bruise or prick $\frac{1}{2}$ lb of sloes. Cover with $\frac{3}{4}$ lb of sugar, leave for several days to draw the juice than add 1 pint of gin. Keep well corked for several months shaking occasionally, add some more

* See pages 140 and 152.

gin, about 6 to 8 oz; leave for another month, strain off and bottle.
The Sloe Gin may be too sweet for some palates, in which case the
gin can be increased up to 1 pint.

Fruit Brandies

A large range of liqueurs can be produced from a variety of
fruit juices obtained by covering the fruit with sugar. This draws
the juice and to this is then added a cheap Brandy or Vodka. The
range of fruits to use is large: raspberries, strawberries, blackcurrants, prunes, peaches, apricots. This method is very costly as
all the alcohol has to be added. A much cheaper way of making
liqueurs is to make use of a sweet and strong fruit wine with as
high an alcohol content as possible. This is made by using a high
proportion of fruit and fermenting on the pulp with the addition
of a pectic enzyme but omitting the Campden tablets. Up to 6 lb
of fruit to the gallon can be used and sugar is added in stages,
enough to produce a sweet wine. As liqueurs are much sweeter than
wines can possibly be, in making the liqueur from a wine more
sugar and alcohol have to be added. It is best to start with half a
pint of wine and stir into this 5 oz of castor sugar. The volume of
the wine will now be increased to 13 oz. As the alcohol content for
fruit liqueurs is generally above 25 per cent by volume it will
suffice to add to the 13 oz of sweetened wine 2¾ oz of 140° proof
Vodka. The liqueur may require additional flavour and 1 to 2
teaspoons of the appropriate flavour will produce a most delicious
liqueur. For red fruit liqueurs such as Cherry Brandy a sweet red
wine should be used. It does not need to be a cherry wine as the
liqueur flavourings are sufficiently strong and in fact elderberry
wine makes an excellent Cherry Brandy. Recipes for several well-
known types of liqueurs are given including the required amount of
alcohol to bring them into line with the corresponding commercial liqueurs, but it is advocated that the amount of alcohol
should be reduced to lower the cost of the liqueur. It must be
emphasized that the flavours mentioned refer to Grey Owl
Flavours. There are indifferent imitations on the market which do
not give the same result.

For those interested in the comparison between alcohol by
volume and Proof Spirit, a table is given in the author's book
Amateur Wine Making (Faber & Faber).

Aperitives and Liqueurs

Apricot Brandy (43° proof)

	BRITISH	U.S.A.	METRIC
Apricot wine sweet	10 oz	10 oz	½ litre
Sugar	5 oz	5 oz	¼ kilo
Vodka 140° proof (80% alcohol)	2¾ oz	2¾ oz	150 ml
Apricot Brandy flavour	1 teasp.	1 teasp.	1 teasp.

Cherry Brandy (43° proof)

	BRITISH	U.S.A.	METRIC
Red Elderberry Wine Port-type	10 oz	10 oz	½ litre
Sugar	5 oz	5 oz	¼ kilo
Vodka 140° proof	2¾ oz	2¾ oz	150 mil
Cherry Brandy Flavour	1 teasp.	1 teasp.	1 teasp.

Crème de Menthe (52° proof)

	BRITISH	U.S.A.	METRIC
Sweet white wine	10 oz	10 oz	½ litre
Sugar	5 oz	5 oz	¼ kilo
Vodka 140° proof	4½ oz	4½ oz	¼ litre
Oil of Peppermint & green food colour	a few drops	a few drops	a few drops
or Crème de Menthe Flavour	1 teasp.	1 teasp.	1 teasp.

Crème d' Anise (52° proof)

	BRITISH	U.S.A.	METRIC
Sweet white wine	10 oz	10 oz	½ litre
Sugar	5 oz	5 oz	¼ kilo
Vodka 140° proof	4½ oz	4½ oz	¼ litre
Anise Flavour	2 teasp.	2 teasp.	2 teasp.

Aperitives and Liqueurs

Crème de Fraise (52° proof)

	BRITISH	U.S.A.	METRIC
Strawberries, mash	½ lb	½ lb	400 gm
and leave overnight with			
Sugar	5 oz	5 oz	¼ kilo
Make up with sweet			
Strawberry Wine to	15 oz	15 oz	¾ litre
Vodka 140° proof	7 oz	7 oz	375 ml

This will be approximately 52° proof.

Similar crème liqueurs can be made from blackcurrants, raspberries, bilberries and blackberries.

Next come crème liqueurs such as Crème de Caffee (or Cafe), Crème de Cocoa (or Cacao). These have a similar alcohol content to the strawberry or other fruit crèmes, but instead of fruit a strong brew of cocoa or coffee extract is used. Some coffee liqueurs have a rum flavour and it is now possible to buy rum of a higher and more suitable alcohol content, namely Grant's 100° proof.

Coffee Rum Liqueur (55° proof)

Brew a very strong coffee and to 5 oz of this add 8 oz of sugar. This will bring the volume up to 10 oz approximately, add 1 oz of coffee essence, a pinch of salt and 13¼ oz of 100° proof Rum. This will bring it to 55° proof like the commercial coffee liqueurs. Add 2 teaspoons of Coffee Rum Flavour.

Next in alcoholic strength are the orange-based liqueurs. Some are made by distillation which is not permissible without an Excise Licence. Others are made by maceration, that means soaking the peel in the strong alcohol/wine mixture. No definite time for soaking can be laid down. Tangerine peel should be chopped and oranges must be grated. Many such liqueurs have an alcohol strength of 52° proof but some, like Curaçao, may go up to 68° and 70° proof. Orange-based liqueurs vary in flavour with the peel used and whether simple orange or curaçao flavours are added. The recipe is identical with that for Crème de Menthe.

Orange Liqueur

	BRITISH	U.S.A.	METRIC
Sweet white wine	10 oz	10 oz	½ litre
Sugar	4–5 oz	4–5 oz	¼ kilo
Vodka 140° proof	4–4½ oz	4–4½ oz	250 ml

The peel is soaked in this and when sufficiently flavoured the peel is removed. If desired either Orange or Curaçao Flavour is added.

Now we come to the more potent liqueurs; commercial examples are Bénédictine (spices and herbs) 75° proof, Pernod (Anise) 70° proof (this is also used as an aperitif), Strega 75° proof, Yellow Chartreuse 75° proof, Green Chartreuse 96° proof. By and large these liqueurs are too expensive for the amateur to make in strengths such as these as it is the alcohol which costs. The appropriate flavours can be used to give liqueurs of equal interest and digestive value even if with a lower alcohol content. The recipe given for Orange Liqueur can be used and the appropriate powder flavour soaked in the sweetened and fortified wine or added as a liquid flavour.

The foregoing recipes for aperitives and liqueurs with some possible variants show that by using sweet wines and moderate additions of alcohol many comparatively inexpensive liqueurs of quality can be made by the amateur. It is of course possible to increase the alcohol content of a wine by freezing out some of the water and straining off the sludge of ice which will retain some of the wine flavour. This can be returned to a freshly fermenting wine. The liquid drained off may contain as much as 25 per cent alcohol, i.e. 58° proof, especially if the freezing is done a second time. Such an alcoholic wine is cheaper to convert into a liqueur. The compounding of aperitives and liqueurs is largely a matter of trial and error and constant tasting until an attractive result is obtained. It will depend very much on the quality of the base wine how a liqueur finally turns out.

16

The Showing and Judging
of Wines

It takes a little courage to submit a wine for judging in a competition for the first time, but everybody goes through this phase. The thing to remember is that having your wines judged and preferably commented on is the best possible way to learn. If it is a competition where the judge merely announces the winners, then ask him for his comments on your wine and make a point whenever possible of getting a taste of the winning ones.

For a beginner the best type of competition is where everyone tastes the wine but a competent judge gives the comments. It is surprising how similar the comments of experienced judges on a single wine will be, while inexperienced judges may differ widely. The reason is that everyone has his own personal preference and these can affect the judgment; but as experience grows allowances for these preferences tend to be made. However, it is highly desirable that judges should be asked to judge the classes for which they have a preference. Wines should always be divided into classes, even for club competitions, so that the exhibitor is forced to prejudge his wine and enter it in the right class.

When entering wine for a competition it is most important to study the schedule. Some shows ask for the wines to be presented in white punted wine bottles fitted with a flanged cork which may be tied down but not held down by either a metal capsule or a viscose cap. This is reasonable in the case of large shows where it is almost impossible to cope with removing capsules or extracting corks. Nevertheless capsules or viscose caps make a bottle look very attractive and I would advise their use for all show benches unless otherwise directed. Furthermore it is desirable to mature the wine in a bottle fitted with a straight-sided cork, and only insert a flanged cork, if the schedule says so, just prior to showing. The wine should practically reach the base of the cork. It is very important to label the bottle as directed in the schedule, as failure to do so may lead some judges to eliminate the wine from the competition. Needless to say the bottle should be clean and preferably water white. Some punted bottles have a slightly green tinge.

When judging wines the very first point which is noted is clarity; this can be achieved by fining the wine. The next is stability and the judge can only check that it is stable at the time he examines it and not whether it will be stable later. It is therefore next to criminal to put a young wine, whether it is fined or not, into a bottle the day before the show. To the judge it may appear stable but after a few hours in a warm room it could become hazy and even blow its cork by the end of the day. This is a disservice to the judge and to the winemaking fraternity, as the uninitiated think the judge incompetent and amateur winemakers incapable of making stable wines. Wines submitted to the National Honey Show have to be in bottle for two months prior to the Show. This rule could well be adopted for all wine competitions.

Another reason why wine should not be re-bottled just prior to the Show is to prevent a wine exhibiting 'bottle sickness'. This occurs in all wines as the aeration which takes place during bottling spoils the flavour *temporarily*. At least a fortnight will be needed for the wine to recover from this temporary aeration, and it may even be longer.

One of the most common faults in amateur wines is a result of the high alcohol content many winemakers try to achieve. By following recipes where the fruit content is high, say about 6 lb to the gallon, or where cereals and bananas are added for good measure, the wine must be high in alcohol and frequently extremely harsh in flavour. Adding water to such wines at the time of consumption markedly improves them, as I have been able to demonstrate on many occasions. It is quite usual to find that Frenchmen add water to their wine before drinking, as this brings out the flavour of the wine which is so easily masked by the high concentration of alcohol. Strongly alcoholic wines can be improved by the addition of water, and if the wines are completely dry then no re-fermentation will take place. If they are sweet then adding water can lead to re-fermentation so the wine must be racked to stabliize it as soon as a yeast deposit is noted.

As indicated previously many wines, particularly dry white wines, are more attractive if served cool. So perhaps it is hardly fair when such wines are judged in the same class against dry red wines which are at their best at room temperature. However, if it is known that judging will be soon after the wines are handed in, then surely there is no harm in making use of such knowledge. It is particularly applicable to a white wine that is somewhat dry and high in acid.

Judging is not an easy task, particularly if the classes are big. However experienced the judge his palate must tire or become fatigued at some stage. If the class is small this is not a serious problem and he can give full attention to each wine in turn. But the judge can be presented with up to two hundred and fifty wines, as has happened to me. Then, in my opinion, there is only one way to tackle the job—that is to go rapidly through the lot, taking a quick taste and spitting out all the wine. By pulling out all the best wines the judge can give a critical appraisement before his palate is fatigued and the others, which are not in the winning positions, can then be conscientiously, even if not so critically, assessed since by that time the judge may suffer from a fatigued palate. If the judge goes through the whole class from beginning to end tasting each wine, he may easily meet the better wines towards the end when he is unable to recognize the quality of the particular wine. In making the final judgment it is desirable, whenever possible, to get another judge to taste a number of the best wines selected and help in classifying these for the awards.

To learn to be a good judge takes years of wine tasting and drinking of commercial wines. Only those with a good palate and considerable experience of commercial wines should go in for judging. Where this is the case comparable conclusions will be reached by different judges. However, judging is fun and it is never too early to start to acquire experience which can best be gained by assisting trained judges and by tasting all wines submitted for competition.

146

17

Your Queries Answered

1. Over the years the most common query I have received has been about the cause of *haziness* in wines. Inspection of the sample received in nine cases out of ten showed that the haze was due to pectin, and on the other occasions was due to bacterial spoilage through the use of an unsuitable yeast. It is quite easy to test the wine for pectin contamination, see page 53. Bacterial spoilage often can be confirmed by holding the wine in front of a lighted candle in a darkened room. A shimmering haze is often due to bacteria and is frequently accompanied by off flavours.

2. Sometimes the query has been—can I sell my wine or give it away to be raffled? Both are illegal. Neither wine nor beer may be sold unless it has been produced under licence and under Excise Control. In such a case duty is charged.

3. Another frequent complaint is that the wine will keep on fermenting. This can be due to an undue proportion of foodstuffs or nutrient in the juice which the yeast cannot absorb during normal fermentation. If racking does not stabilize the wine then it has to be pasteurized, see page 62.

4. Yet another complaint is that the fermentation had stuck. The winemaker started with plenty of food and sugar and the fermentation had stopped while the wine was still sweet. Inspection of the wine in a glass showed that the wine was quite alcoholic, as alcohol crept up the side of the glass. A chemical analysis showed an alcohol content of 15 per cent. This, of course, was the maximum the yeast could tolerate and this was therefore not a

sticking fermentation but a completed one. If the wine was too sweet it could either be used for blending or the fermentation could be made to continue. Provided that the wine had not been racked off from the yeast deposit a pint of water added to the gallon would allow the yeast to resume fermentation.

5. A further complaint was that the fermentation stopped after a few days. This could be due to two causes; an unsuitable yeast or too high an initial sugar concentration. It would be best to stir up any residue and to transfer some of the juice to a small bottle and add half as much water. If fermentation ensued then the fault was due to an undesirable sugar concentration, and could be cured by adding one or two pints of water to the gallon. If the trouble was due to an unsuitable yeast, subsequent addition of a purer yeast may prove a remedy; but prevention is better than cure.

6. Some winemakers do not seem certain how much or how little yeast to add to the starter bottle or the fermenting vessel. It does not really matter as the yeast will find its own level. The more is added the quicker will the fermentation start, but the total amount of yeast that will grow is roughly the same. How much will grow depends on the amount of food present in the juice. The amount of yeast on an agar slant will be sufficient to start one gallon fermenting in 24 to 36 hours, while a liquid yeast with a good deposit in the phial will do the same. On the other hand, half a liquid yeast suffices for 1 gallon. Unless the yeast starts in a starter bottle in 24 hours it is likely to be grossly impure.

7. Complaints have been received that yeasts in a starter bottle would not ferment although the bottle was shaken daily. This shaking was, of course, the reason why the yeast could not ferment. Agitation or aeration causes yeast growth. Leaving undisturbed allows the yeast first to charge the juice with gas, and after this fermentation starts.

8. Another interesting query was that the fermenting wines after being moved ceased to ferment. The reason is the same as in the previous query but as the juice had already been fermenting for some time, patience is the only remedy. After some weeks fermentation may re-ensue, but prevention is better than cure.

9. A question sometimes asked is why fermentation stops after racking. Well, this should be self-evident. As it is the yeast which causes the fermentation, by taking it off the yeast, fermentation must stop. It may start again later after some more yeast has grown.

148

Your Queries Answered

10. Another query is that the gravity of a wine does not drop yet gas is evolved. This is generally due to a period of renewed yeast growth. The yeast absorbs the sugar and the proteins and as it does so carbon dioxide gas is evolved.

11. Sometimes complaints are made that the once clear wine has gone slightly hazy. This is nearly always due to renewed yeast growth.

12. Finally—why has my wine darkened? Almost certainly because it has been exposed to air when it should not have been, and it had not had added to it sufficient sulphite (Campden tablets) to use up the oxygen. The same problem occurs in commercial wines but there is more excuse when large volumes have to be handled. Alternatively, wines made from mouldy fruit tend to darken unless more than the normal number of Campden tablets are added.

Conclusion

It has been the aim in this book to guide the winemaker by easy stages and ensure that sound methods are learnt and understood. By following the advice given on racking and sulphiting, the winemaker will automatically nurse his wine to perfection. Although winemaking by amateurs has only gained the impetus it has since the abolition of sugar rationing, it is amazing how much has been learned and understood within recent years. Also owing to the publication of much basic technical information there has been a growing interest in the *technique* of winemaking; hence there has been a tendency to become more and more scientific and to forget that winemaking is really an art. Science helps in understanding what happens but cannot replace the skill of the vintner. The *art* of winemaking can be learned without a scientific background, but whether the art or the science is practised it is equally important to be able to assess wine quality through the development of a palate. This can only be done by drinking and tasting commercial wines and comparing them with home-produced wines. It is in fact quite amazing how fruit wines properly made and matured can resemble some of the lesser grape wines, and how skilful experienced amateur wine makers have become in producing such wines.

This does not mean that I decry the desire to study and understand fundamentals. A good winemaker who has a basic knowledge of the technical and scientific principles of winemaking cannot but become a better winemaker. He will understand why some methods he has adopted give better results than others. All this makes for lively discussion and accordingly increases the zest for good wine and winemaking.

Conclusion

Finally, I take off my hat to all those who make wine and aim for perfection and to the many devoted winemakers who have organized National Wine Conferences and Competitions and have given their time and energy to help in improving the standards of amateur winemaking. It has become a most absorbing hobby to so many, and the numbers are continually increasing; but of equal importance are the good fellowship encountered in Wine Circles and the many friends made through a community of interest.

List of American Suppliers

As winemaking equipment and ingredients were, at one time, not freely available it has become the custom in books of this sort to include a list of suppliers. This has now become so large that only a few of the larger firms are mentioned here.

Wine Art of America, 301 South Kressen St., Baltimore, Maryland 21224.

Wine Art of America, 4324 Geary Blvd., San Francisco, California 94118.

(There are over 100 Wine Art stores throughout the U.S.)

Hobby Winemaking, Inc., 2758 N.E. Broadway, Portland, Oregon 97232.

Aetna Bottle Co., 708 Rainier Avenue South, Seattle, Washington 98144.

F. H. Steinbart, 526 S.E. Grand Portland Ave., Portland, Oregon 97214.

Jim's Home Beverage, North 2613 Division, Spokane, Washington 99207.

The Winemakers Shop, Bully Hill Farms, R.D. 2, Hammondsport, New York 14840.

The Compleat Winemaker, P.O. Box 2470, Yountville, California 94599.

Index

Index

Index

Index

A CATALOGUE OF
SELECTED DOVER BOOKS
IN ALL FIELDS OF INTEREST

A CATALOGUE OF SELECTED DOVER BOOKS IN ALL FIELDS OF INTEREST

CELESTIAL OBJECTS FOR COMMON TELESCOPES, T. W. Webb. The most used book in amateur astronomy: inestimable aid for locating and identifying nearly 4,000 celestial objects. Edited, updated by Margaret W. Mayall. 77 illustrations. Total of 645pp. 5⅜ x 8½.
20917-2, 20918-0 Pa., Two-vol. set $10.00

HISTORICAL STUDIES IN THE LANGUAGE OF CHEMISTRY, M. P. Crosland. The important part language has played in the development of chemistry from the symbolism of alchemy to the adoption of systematic nomenclature in 1892. ". . . wholeheartedly recommended,"—Science. 15 illustrations. 416pp. of text. 5⅝ x 8¼. 63702-6 Pa. $7.50

BURNHAM'S CELESTIAL HANDBOOK, Robert Burnham, Jr. Thorough, readable guide to the stars beyond our solar system. Exhaustive treatment, fully illustrated. Breakdown is alphabetical by constellation: Andromeda to Cetus in Vol. 1; Chamaeleon to Orion in Vol. 2; and Pavo to Vulpecula in Vol. 3. Hundreds of illustrations. Total of about 2000pp. 6⅛ x 9¼.
23567-X, 23568-8, 23673-0 Pa., Three-vol. set $32.85

THEORY OF WING SECTIONS: INCLUDING A SUMMARY OF AIRFOIL DATA, Ira H. Abbott and A. E. von Doenhoff. Concise compilation of subatomic aerodynamic characteristics of modern NASA wing sections, plus description of theory. 350pp. of tables. 693pp. 5⅜ x 8½.
60586-8 Pa. $9.95

DE RE METALLICA, Georgius Agricola. Translated by Herbert C. Hoover and Lou H. Hoover. The famous Hoover translation of greatest treatise on technological chemistry, engineering, geology, mining of early modern times (1556). All 289 original woodcuts. 638pp. 6¾ x 11.
60006-8 Clothbd. $19.95

THE ORIGIN OF CONTINENTS AND OCEANS, Alfred Wegener. One of the most influential, most controversial books in science, the classic statement for continental drift. Full 1966 translation of Wegener's final (1929) version. 64 illustrations. 246pp. 5⅜ x 8½. (EBE) 61708-4 Pa. $5.00

THE PRINCIPLES OF PSYCHOLOGY, William James. Famous long course complete, unabridged. Stream of thought, time perception, memory, experimental methods; great work decades ahead of its time. Still valid, useful; read in many classes. 94 figures. Total of 1391pp. 5⅜ x 8½.
20381-6, 20382-4 Pa., Two-vol. set $17.90

CATALOGUE OF DOVER BOOKS

YUCATAN BEFORE AND AFTER THE CONQUEST, Diego de Landa. First English translation of basic book in Maya studies, the only significant account of Yucatan written in the early post-Conquest era. Translated by distinguished Maya scholar William Gates. Appendices, introduction, 4 maps and over 120 illustrations added by translator. 162pp. 5⅜ x 8½.
23622-6 Pa. $3.00

THE MALAY ARCHIPELAGO, Alfred R. Wallace. Spirited travel account by one of founders of modern biology. Touches on zoology, botany, ethnography, geography, and geology. 62 illustrations, maps. 515pp. 5⅜ x 8½.
20187-2 Pa. $6.95

THE DISCOVERY OF THE TOMB OF TUTANKHAMEN, Howard Carter, A. C. Mace. Accompany Carter in the thrill of discovery, as ruined passage suddenly reveals unique, untouched, fabulously rich tomb. Fascinating account, with 106 illustrations. New introduction by J. M. White. Total of 382pp. 5⅜ x 8½. (Available in U.S. only)   23500-9 Pa. $5.50

THE WORLD'S GREATEST SPEECHES, edited by Lewis Copeland and Lawrence W. Lamm. Vast collection of 278 speeches from Greeks up to present. Powerful and effective models; unique look at history. Revised to 1970. Indices. 842pp. 5⅜ x 8½.   20468-5 Pa. $9.95

THE 100 GREATEST ADVERTISEMENTS, Julian Watkins. The priceless ingredient; His master's voice; 99 44/100% pure; over 100 others. How they were written, their impact, etc. Remarkable record. 130 illustrations. 233pp. 7⅞ x 10 3/5.   20540-1 Pa. $6.95

CRUICKSHANK PRINTS FOR HAND COLORING, George Cruickshank. 18 illustrations, one side of a page, on fine-quality paper suitable for watercolors. Caricatures of people in society (c. 1820) full of trenchant wit. Very large format. 32pp. 11 x 16.   23684-6 Pa. $6.00

THIRTY-TWO COLOR POSTCARDS OF TWENTIETH-CENTURY AMERICAN ART, Whitney Museum of American Art. Reproduced in full color in postcard form are 31 art works and one shot of the museum. Calder, Hopper, Rauschenberg, others. Detachable. 16pp. 8¼ x 11.
23629-3 Pa. $3.50

MUSIC OF THE SPHERES: THE MATERIAL UNIVERSE FROM ATOM TO QUASAR SIMPLY EXPLAINED, Guy Murchie. Planets, stars, geology, atoms, radiation, relativity, quantum theory, light, antimatter, similar topics. 319 figures. 664pp. 5⅜ x 8½.
21809-0, 21810-4 Pa., Two-vol. set $11.00

EINSTEIN'S THEORY OF RELATIVITY, Max Born. Finest semi-technical account; covers Einstein, Lorentz, Minkowski, and others, with much detail, much explanation of ideas and math not readily available elsewhere on this level. For student, non-specialist. 376pp. 5⅜ x 8½.
60769-0 Pa. $5.00

THE SENSE OF BEAUTY, George Santayana. Masterfully written discussion of nature of beauty, materials of beauty, form, expression; art, literature, social sciences all involved. 168pp. 5⅜ x 8½. 20238-0 Pa. $3.50

ON THE IMPROVEMENT OF THE UNDERSTANDING, Benedict Spinoza. Also contains *Ethics, Correspondence,* all in excellent R. Elwes translation. Basic works on entry to philosophy, pantheism, exchange of ideas with great contemporaries. 402pp. 5⅜ x 8½. 20250-X Pa. $5.95

THE TRAGIC SENSE OF LIFE, Miguel de Unamuno. Acknowledged masterpiece of existential literature, one of most important books of 20th century. Introduction by Madariaga. 367pp. 5⅜ x 8½.
20257-7 Pa. $6.00

THE GUIDE FOR THE PERPLEXED, Moses Maimonides. Great classic of medieval Judaism attempts to reconcile revealed religion (Pentateuch, commentaries) with Aristotelian philosophy. Important historically, still relevant in problems. Unabridged Friedlander translation. Total of 473pp. 5⅜ x 8½. 20351-4 Pa. $6.95

THE I CHING (THE BOOK OF CHANGES), translated by James Legge. Complete translation of basic text plus appendices by Confucius, and Chinese commentary of most penetrating divination manual ever prepared. Indispensable to study of early Oriental civilizations, to modern inquiring reader. 448pp. 5⅜ x 8½. 21062-6 Pa. $6.00

THE EGYPTIAN BOOK OF THE DEAD, E. A. Wallis Budge. Complete reproduction of Ani's papyrus, finest ever found. Full hieroglyphic text, interlinear transliteration, word for word translation, smooth translation. Basic work, for Egyptology, for modern study of psychic matters. Total of 533pp. 6½ x 9¼. (USCO) 21866-X Pa. $8.50

THE GODS OF THE EGYPTIANS, E. A. Wallis Budge. Never excelled for richness, fullness: all gods, goddesses, demons, mythical figures of Ancient Egypt; their legends, rites, incarnations, variations, powers, etc. Many hieroglyphic texts cited. Over 225 illustrations, plus 6 color plates. Total of 988pp. 6⅛ x 9¼. (EBE)
22055-9, 22056-7 Pa., Two-vol. set $20.00

THE STANDARD BOOK OF QUILT MAKING AND COLLECTING, Marguerite Ickis. Full information, full-sized patterns for making 46 traditional quilts, also 150 other patterns. Quilted cloths, lame, satin quilts, etc. 483 illustrations. 273pp. 6⅞ x 9⅝. 20582-7 Pa. $5.95

CORAL GARDENS AND THEIR MAGIC, Bronsilaw Malinowski. Classic study of the methods of tilling the soil and of agricultural rites in the Trobriand Islands of Melanesia. Author is one of the most important figures in the field of modern social anthropology. 143 illustrations. Indexes. Total of 911pp. of text. 5⅝ x 8¼. (Available in U.S. only)
23597-1 Pa. $12.95

THE PHILOSOPHY OF HISTORY, Georg W. Hegel. Great classic of Western thought develops concept that history is not chance but a rational process, the evolution of freedom. 457pp. 5⅜ x 8½.　20112-0 Pa. $6.00

LANGUAGE, TRUTH AND LOGIC, Alfred J. Ayer. Famous, clear introduction to Vienna, Cambridge schools of Logical Positivism. Role of philosophy, elimination of metaphysics, nature of analysis, etc. 160pp. 5⅜ x 8½. (USCO)　20010-8 Pa. $2.50

A PREFACE TO LOGIC, Morris R. Cohen. Great City College teacher in renowned, easily followed exposition of formal logic, probability, values, logic and world order and similar topics; no previous background needed. 209pp. 5⅜ x 8½.　23517-3 Pa. $4.95

REASON AND NATURE, Morris R. Cohen. Brilliant analysis of reason and its multitudinous ramifications by charismatic teacher. Interdisciplinary, synthesizing work widely praised when it first appeared in 1931. Second (1953) edition. Indexes. 496pp. 5⅜ x 8½.　23633-1 Pa. $7.50

AN ESSAY CONCERNING HUMAN UNDERSTANDING, John Locke. The only complete edition of enormously important classic, with authoritative editorial material by A. C. Fraser. Total of 1176pp. 5⅜ x 8½.
20530-4, 20531-2 Pa., Two-vol. set $16.00

HANDBOOK OF MATHEMATICAL FUNCTIONS WITH FORMULAS, GRAPHS, AND MATHEMATICAL TABLES, edited by Milton Abramowitz and Irene A. Stegun. Vast compendium: 29 sets of tables, some to as high as 20 places. 1,046pp. 8 x 10½.　61272-4 Pa. $17.95

MATHEMATICS FOR THE PHYSICAL SCIENCES, Herbert S. Wilf. Highly acclaimed work offers clear presentations of vector spaces and matrices, orthogonal functions, roots of polynomial equations, conformal mapping, calculus of variations, etc. Knowledge of theory of. functions of real and complex variables is assumed. Exercises and solutions. Index. 284pp. 5⅝ x 8¼.　63635-6 Pa. $5.00

THE PRINCIPLE OF RELATIVITY, Albert Einstein et al. Eleven most important original papers on special and general theories. Seven by Einstein, two by Lorentz, one each by Minkowski and Weyl. All translated, unabridged. 216pp. 5⅜ x 8½.　60081-5 Pa. $3.50

THERMODYNAMICS, Enrico Fermi. A classic of modern science. Clear, organized treatment of systems, first and second laws, entropy, thermodynamic potentials, gaseous reactions, dilute solutions, entropy constant. No math beyond calculus required. Problems. 160pp. 5⅜ x 8½.
60361-X Pa. $4.00

ELEMENTARY MECHANICS OF FLUIDS, Hunter Rouse. Classic undergraduate text widely considered to be far better than many later books. Ranges from fluid velocity and acceleration to role of compressibility in fluid motion. Numerous examples, questions, problems. 224 illustrations. 376pp. 5⅝ x 8¼.　63699-2 Pa. $7.00

THE AMERICAN SENATOR, Anthony Trollope. Little known, long unavailable Trollope novel on a grand scale. Here are humorous comment on American vs. English culture, and stunning portrayal of a heroine/villainess. Superb evocation of Victorian village life. 561pp. 5⅜ x 8½.
23801-6 Pa. $7.95

WAS IT MURDER? James Hilton. The author of *Lost Horizon* and *Goodbye, Mr. Chips* wrote one detective novel (under a pen-name) which was quickly forgotten and virtually lost, even at the height of Hilton's fame. This edition brings it back—a finely crafted public school puzzle resplendent with Hilton's stylish atmosphere. A thoroughly English thriller by the creator of Shangri-la. 252pp. 5⅜ x 8. (Available in U.S. only)
23774-5 Pa. $3.00

CENTRAL PARK: A PHOTOGRAPHIC GUIDE, Victor Laredo and Henry Hope Reed. 121 superb photographs show dramatic views of Central Park: Bethesda Fountain, Cleopatra's Needle, Sheep Meadow, the Blockhouse, plus people engaged in many park activities: ice skating, bike riding, etc. Captions by former Curator of Central Park, Henry Hope Reed, provide historical view, changes, etc. Also photos of N.Y. landmarks on park's periphery. 96pp. 8½ x 11. 23750-8 Pa. $4.50

NANTUCKET IN THE NINETEENTH CENTURY, Clay Lancaster. 180 rare photographs, stereographs, maps, drawings and floor plans recreate unique American island society. Authentic scenes of shipwreck, lighthouses, streets, homes are arranged in geographic sequence to provide walking-tour guide to old Nantucket existing today. Introduction, captions. 160pp. 8⅞ x 11¾. 23747-8 Pa. $7.95

STONE AND MAN: A PHOTOGRAPHIC EXPLORATION, Andreas Feininger. 106 photographs by *Life* photographer Feininger portray man's deep passion for stone through the ages. Stonehenge-like megaliths, fortified towns, sculpted marble and crumbling tenements show textures, beauties, fascination. 128pp. 9¼ x 10¾. 23756-7 Pa. $5.95

CIRCLES, A MATHEMATICAL VIEW, D. Pedoe. Fundamental aspects of college geometry, non-Euclidean geometry, and other branches of mathematics: representing circle by point. Poincare model, isoperimetric property, etc. Stimulating recreational reading. 66 figures. 96pp. 5⅝ x 8¼.
63698-4 Pa. $3.50

THE DISCOVERY OF NEPTUNE, Morton Grosser. Dramatic scientific history of the investigations leading up to the actual discovery of the eighth planet of our solar system. Lucid, well-researched book by well-known historian of science. 172pp. 5⅜ x 8½. 23726-5 Pa. $3.50

THE DEVIL'S DICTIONARY. Ambrose Bierce. Barbed, bitter, brilliant witticisms in the form of a dictionary. Best, most ferocious satire America has produced. 145pp. 5⅜ x 8½. 20487-1 Pa. $2.50

HISTORY OF BACTERIOLOGY, William Bulloch. The only comprehensive history of bacteriology from the beginnings through the 19th century. Special emphasis is given to biography-Leeuwenhoek, etc. Brief accounts of 350 bacteriologists form a separate section. No clearer, fuller study, suitable to scientists and general readers, has yet been written. 52 illustrations. 448pp. 5⅝ x 8¼. 23761-3 Pa. $6.50

THE COMPLETE NONSENSE OF EDWARD LEAR, Edward Lear. All nonsense limericks, zany alphabets, Owl and Pussycat, songs, nonsense botany, etc., illustrated by Lear. Total of 321pp. 5⅜ x 8½. (Available in U.S. only) 20167-8 Pa. $4.50

INGENIOUS MATHEMATICAL PROBLEMS AND METHODS, Louis A. Graham. Sophisticated material from Graham *Dial,* applied and pure; stresses solution methods. Logic, number theory, networks, inversions, etc. 237pp. 5⅜ x 8½. 20545-2 Pa. $4.50

BEST MATHEMATICAL PUZZLES OF SAM LOYD, edited by Martin Gardner. Bizarre, original, whimsical puzzles by America's greatest puzzler. From fabulously rare *Cyclopedia,* including famous 14-15 puzzles, the Horse of a Different Color, 115 more. Elementary math. 150 illustrations. 167pp. 5⅜ x 8½. 20498-7 Pa. $3.50

THE BASIS OF COMBINATION IN CHESS, J. du Mont. Easy-to-follow, instructive book on elements of combination play, with chapters on each piece and every powerful combination team—two knights, bishop and knight, rook and bishop, etc. 250 diagrams. 218pp. 5⅜ x 8½. (Available in U.S. only) 23644-7 Pa. $4.50

MODERN CHESS STRATEGY, Ludek Pachman. The use of the queen, the active king, exchanges, pawn play, the center, weak squares, etc. Section on rook alone worth price of the book. Stress on the moderns. Often considered the most important book on strategy. 314pp. 5⅜ x 8½. 20290-9 Pa. $5.00

LASKER'S MANUAL OF CHESS, Dr. Emanuel Lasker. Great world champion offers very thorough coverage of all aspects of chess. Combinations, position play, openings, end game, aesthetics of chess, philosophy of struggle, much more. Filled with analyzed games. 390pp. 5⅜ x 8½. 20640-8 Pa. $5.95

500 MASTER GAMES OF CHESS, S. Tartakower, J. du Mont. Vast collection of great chess games from 1798-1938, with much material nowhere else readily available. Fully annotated, arranged by opening for easier study. 664pp. 5⅜ x 8½. 23208-5 Pa. $8.50

A GUIDE TO CHESS ENDINGS, Dr. Max Euwe, David Hooper. One of the finest modern works on chess endings. Thorough analysis of the most frequently encountered endings by former world champion. 331 examples, each with diagram. 248pp. 5⅜ x 8½. 23332-4 Pa. $3.95

THE COMPLETE BOOK OF DOLL MAKING AND COLLECTING, Catherine Christopher. Instructions, patterns for dozens of dolls, from rag doll on up to elaborate, historically accurate figures. Mould faces, sew clothing, make doll houses, etc. Also collecting information. Many illustrations. 288pp. 6 x 9. 22066-4 Pa. $4.95

THE DAGUERREOTYPE IN AMERICA, Beaumont Newhall. Wonderful portraits, 1850's townscapes, landscapes; full text plus 104 photographs. The basic book. Enlarged 1976 edition. 272pp. 8¼ x 11¼. 23322-7 Pa. $7.95

CRAFTSMAN HOMES, Gustav Stickley. 296 architectural drawings, floor plans, and photographs illustrate 40 different kinds of "Mission-style" homes from The Craftsman (1901-16), voice of American style of simplicity and organic harmony. Thorough coverage of Craftsman idea in text and picture, now collector's item. 224pp. 8⅛ x 11. 23791-5 Pa. $6.50

PEWTER-WORKING: INSTRUCTIONS AND PROJECTS, Burl N. Osborn. & Gordon O. Wilber. Introduction to pewter-working for amateur craftsman. History and characteristics of pewter; tools, materials, step-by-step instructions. Photos, line drawings, diagrams. Total of 160pp. 7⅞ x 10¾. 23786-9 Pa. $3.50

THE GREAT CHICAGO FIRE, edited by David Lowe. 10 dramatic, eyewitness accounts of the 1871 disaster, including one of the aftermath and rebuilding, plus 70 contemporary photographs and illustrations of the ruins—courthouse, Palmer House, Great Central Depot, etc. Introduction by David Lowe. 87pp. 8¼ x 11. 23771-0 Pa. $4.00

SILHOUETTES: A PICTORIAL ARCHIVE OF VARIED ILLUSTRATIONS, edited by Carol Belanger Grafton. Over 600 silhouettes from the 18th to 20th centuries include profiles and full figures of men and women, children, birds and animals, groups and scenes, nature, ships, an alphabet. Dozens of uses for commercial artists and craftspeople. 144pp. 8⅜ x 11¼. 23781-8 Pa. $4.50

ANIMALS: 1,419 COPYRIGHT-FREE ILLUSTRATIONS OF MAMMALS, BIRDS, FISH, INSECTS, ETC., edited by Jim Harter. Clear wood engravings present, in extremely lifelike poses, over 1,000 species of animals. One of the most extensive copyright-free pictorial sourcebooks of its kind. Captions. Index. 284pp. 9 x 12. 23766-4 Pa. $8.95

INDIAN DESIGNS FROM ANCIENT ECUADOR, Frederick W. Shaffer. 282 original designs by pre-Columbian Indians of Ecuador (500-1500 A.D.). Designs include people, mammals, birds, reptiles, fish, plants, heads, geometric designs. Use as is or alter for advertising, textiles, leathercraft, etc. Introduction. 95pp. 8¾ x 11¼. 23764-8 Pa. $4.50

SZIGETI ON THE VIOLIN, Joseph Szigeti. Genial, loosely structured tour by premier violinist, featuring a pleasant mixture of reminiscenes, insights into great music and musicians, innumerable tips for practicing violinists. 385 musical passages. 256pp. 5⅝ x 8¼. 23763-X Pa. $4.00

TONE POEMS, SERIES II: TILL EULENSPIEGELS LUSTIGE STREICHE, ALSO SPRACH ZARATHUSTRA, AND EIN HELDEN-LEBEN, Richard Strauss. Three important orchestral works, including very popular *Till Eulenspiegel's Marry Pranks*, reproduced in full score from original editions. Study score. 315pp. 9⅜ x 12¼. (Available in U.S. only) 23755-9 Pa. $8.95

TONE POEMS, SERIES I: DON JUAN, TOD UND VERKLARUNG AND DON QUIXOTE, Richard Strauss. Three of the most often performed and recorded works in entire orchestral repertoire, reproduced in full score from original editions. Study score. 286pp. 9⅜ x 12¼. (Available in U.S. only) 23754-0 Pa. $8.95

11 LATE STRING QUARTETS, Franz Joseph Haydn. The form which Haydn defined and "brought to perfection." (*Grove's*). 11 string quartets in complete score, his last and his best. The first in a projected series of the complete Haydn string quartets. Reliable modern Eulenberg edition, otherwise difficult to obtain. 320pp. 8⅜ x 11¼. (Available in U.S. only) 23753-2 Pa. $8.95

FOURTH, FIFTH AND SIXTH SYMPHONIES IN FULL SCORE, Peter Ilyitch Tchaikovsky. Complete orchestral scores of Symphony No. 4 in F Minor, Op. 36; Symphony No. 5 in E Minor, Op. 64; Symphony No. 6 in B Minor, "Pathetique," Op. 74. Bretikopf & Hartel eds. Study score. 480pp. 9⅜ x 12¼. 23861-X Pa. $10.95

THE MARRIAGE OF FIGARO: COMPLETE SCORE, Wolfgang A. Mozart. Finest comic opera ever written. Full score, not to be confused with piano renderings. Peters edition. Study score. 448pp. 9⅜ x 12¼. (Available in U.S. only) 23751-6 Pa. $12.95

"IMAGE" ON THE ART AND EVOLUTION OF THE FILM, edited by Marshall Deutelbaum. Pioneering book brings together for first time 38 groundbreaking articles on early silent films from *Image* and 263 illustrations newly shot from rare prints in the collection of the International Museum of Photography. A landmark work. Index. 256pp. 8¼ x 11. 23777-X Pa. $8.95

AROUND-THE-WORLD COOKY BOOK, Lois Lintner Sumption and Marguerite Lintner Ashbrook. 373 cooky and frosting recipes from 28 countries (America, Austria, China, Russia, Italy, etc.) include Viennese kisses, rice wafers, London strips, lady fingers, hony, sugar spice, maple cookies, etc. Clear instructions. All tested. 38 drawings. 182pp. 5⅜ x 8. 23802-4 Pa. $2.75

THE ART NOUVEAU STYLE, edited by Roberta Waddell. 579 rare photographs, not available elsewhere, of works in jewelry, metalwork, glass, ceramics, textiles, architecture and furniture by 175 artists—Mucha, Seguy, Lalique, Tiffany, Gaudin, Hohlwein, Saarinen, and many others. 288pp. 8⅜ x 11¼. 23515-7 Pa. $8.95

THE CURVES OF LIFE, Theodore A. Cook. Examination of shells, leaves, horns, human body, art, etc., in "*the* classic reference on how the golden ratio applies to spirals and helices in nature . . . . "—Martin Gardner. 426 illustrations. Total of 512pp. 5⅜ x 8½. 23701-X Pa. $6.95

AN ILLUSTRATED FLORA OF THE NORTHERN UNITED STATES AND CANADA, Nathaniel L. Britton, Addison Brown. Encyclopedic work covers 4666 species, ferns on up. Everything. Full botanical information, illustration for each. This earlier edition is preferred by many to more recent revisions. 1913 edition. Over 4000 illustrations, total of 2087pp. 6⅛ x 9¼. 22642-5, 22643-3, 22644-1 Pa., Three-vol. set $28.50

MANUAL OF THE GRASSES OF THE UNITED STATES, A. S. Hitchcock, U.S. Dept. of Agriculture. The basic study of American grasses, both indigenous and escapes, cultivated and wild. Over 1400 species. Full descriptions, information. Over 1100 maps, illustrations. Total of 1051pp. 5⅜ x 8½. 22717-0, 22718-9 Pa., Two-vol. set $17.00

THE CACTACEAE,, Nathaniel L. Britton, John N. Rose. Exhaustive, definitive. Every cactus in the world. Full botanical descriptions. Thorough statement of nomenclatures, habitat, detailed finding keys. The one book needed by every cactus enthusiast. Over 1275 illustrations. Total of 1080pp. 8 x 10¼. 21191-6, 21192-4 Clothbd., Two-vol. set $50.00

AMERICAN MEDICINAL PLANTS, Charles F. Millspaugh. Full descriptions, 180 plants covered: history; physical description; methods of preparation with all chemical constituents extracted; all claimed curative or adverse effects. 180 full-page plates. Classification table. 804pp. 6½ x 9¼. 23034-1 Pa. $13.95

A MODERN HERBAL, Margaret Grieve. Much the fullest, most exact, most useful compilation of herbal material. Gigantic alphabetical encyclopedia, from aconite to zedoary, gives botanical information, medical properties, folklore, economic uses, and much else. Indispensable to serious reader. 161 illustrations. 888pp. 6½ x 9¼. (Available in U.S. only) 22798-7, 22799-5 Pa., Two-vol. set $15.00

THE HERBAL or GENERAL HISTORY OF PLANTS, John Gerard. The 1633 edition revised and enlarged by Thomas Johnson. Containing almost 2850 plant descriptions and 2705 superb illustrations, Gerard's *Herbal* is a monumental work, the book all modern English herbals are derived from, the one herbal every serious enthusiast should have in its entirety. Original editions are worth perhaps $750. 1678pp. 8½ x 12¼. 23147-X Clothbd. $75.00

MANUAL OF THE TREES OF NORTH AMERICA, Charles S. Sargent. The basic survey of every native tree and tree-like shrub, 717 species in all. Extremely full descriptions, information on habitat, growth, locales, economics, etc. Necessary to every serious tree lover. Over 100 finding keys. 783 illustrations. Total of 986pp. 5⅜ x 8½. 20277-1, 20278-X Pa., Two-vol. set $12.00

GREAT NEWS PHOTOS AND THE STORIES BEHIND THEM, John Faber. Dramatic volume of 140 great news photos, 1855 through 1976, and revealing stories behind them, with both historical and technical information. Hindenburg disaster, shooting of Oswald, nomination of Jimmy Carter, etc. 160pp. 8¼ x 11. 23667-6 Pa. $6.00

CRUICKSHANK'S PHOTOGRAPHS OF BIRDS OF AMERICA, Allan D. Cruickshank. Great ornithologist, photographer presents 177 closeups, groupings, panoramas, flightings, etc., of about 150 different birds. Expanded *Wings in the Wilderness*. Introduction by Helen G. Crujckshank. 191pp. 8¼ x 11. 23497-5 Pa. $7.95

AMERICAN WILDLIFE AND PLANTS, A. C. Martin, et al. Describes food habits of more than 1000 species of mammals, birds, fish. Special treatment of important food plants. Over 300 illustrations. 500pp. 5⅜ x 8½. 20793-5 Pa. $6.50

THE PEOPLE CALLED SHAKERS, Edward D. Andrews. Lifetime of research, definitive study of Shakers: origins, beliefs, practices, dances, social organization, furniture and crafts, impact on 19th-century USA, present heritage. Indispensable to student of American history, collector. 33 illustrations. 351pp. 5⅜ x 8½. 21081-2 Pa. $4.50

OLD NEW YORK IN EARLY PHOTOGRAPHS, Mary Black. New York City as it was in 1853-1901, through 196 wonderful photographs from N.-Y. Historical Society. Great Blizzard, Lincoln's funeral procession, great buildings. 228pp. 9 x 12. 22907-6 Pa. $8.95

MR. LINCOLN'S CAMERA MAN: MATHEW BRADY, Roy Meredith. Over 300 Brady photos reproduced directly from original negatives, photos. Jackson, Webster, Grant, Lee, Carnegie, Barnum; Lincoln; Battle Smoke, Death of Rebel Sniper, Atlanta Just After Capture. Lively commentary. 368pp. 8⅜ x 11¼. 23021-X Pa. $11.95

TRAVELS OF WILLIAM BARTRAM, William Bartram. From 1773-8, Bartram explored Northern Florida, Georgia, Carolinas, and reported on wild life, plants, Indians, early settlers. Basic account for period, entertaining reading. Edited by Mark Van Doren. 13 illustrations. 141pp. 5⅜ x 8½. 20013-2 Pa. $6.00

THE GENTLEMAN AND CABINET MAKER'S DIRECTOR, Thomas Chippendale. Full reprint, 1762 style book, most influential of all time; chairs, tables, sofas, mirrors, cabinets, etc. 200 plates, plus 24 photographs of surviving pieces. 249pp. 9⅞ x 12¾. 21601-2 Pa. $8.95

AMERICAN CARRIAGES, SLEIGHS, SULKIES AND CARTS, edited by Don H. Berkebile. 168 Victorian illustrations from catalogues, trade journals, fully captioned. Useful for artists. Author is Assoc. Curator, Div. of Transportation of Smithsonian Institution. 168pp. 8½ x 9½. 23328-6 Pa. $5.00

SECOND PIATIGORSKY CUP, edited by Isaac Kashdan. One of the greatest tournament books ever produced in the English language. All 90 games of the 1966 tournament, annotated by players, most annotated by both players. Features Petrosian, Spassky, Fischer, Larsen, six others. 228pp. 5⅜ x 8½. 23572-6 Pa. $3.50

ENCYCLOPEDIA OF CARD TRICKS, revised and edited by Jean Hugard. How to perform over 600 card tricks, devised by the world's greatest magicians: impromptus, spelling tricks, key cards, using special packs, much, much more. Additional chapter on card technique. 66 illustrations. 402pp. 5⅜ x 8½. (Available in U.S. only) 21252-1 Pa. $5.95

MAGIC: STAGE ILLUSIONS, SPECIAL EFFECTS AND TRICK PHO-TOGRAPHY, Albert A. Hopkins, Henry R. Evans. One of the great classics; fullest, most authoritive explanation of vanishing lady, levitations, scores of other great stage effects. Also small magic, automata, stunts. 446 illus-trations. 556pp. 5⅜ x 8½. 23344-8 Pa. $6.95

THE SECRETS OF HOUDINI, J. C. Cannell. Classic study of Houdini's incredible magic, exposing closely-kept professional secrets and revealing, in general terms, the whole art of stage magic. 67 illustrations. 279pp. 5⅜ x 8½. 22913-0 Pa. $4.00

HOFFMANN'S MODERN MAGIC, Professor Hoffmann. One of the best, and best-known, magicians' manuals of the past century. Hundreds of tricks from card tricks and simple sleight of hand to elaborate illusions involving construction of complicated machinery. 332 illustrations. 563pp. 5⅜ x 8½. 23623-4 Pa. $6.95

THOMAS NAST'S CHRISTMAS DRAWINGS, Thomas Nast. Almost all Christmas drawings by creator of image of Santa Claus as we know it, and one of America's foremost illustrators and political cartoonists. 66 illustrations. 3 illustrations in color on covers. 96pp. 8⅜ x 11¼. 23660-9 Pa. $3.50

FRENCH COUNTRY COOKING FOR AMERICANS, Louis Diat. 500 easy-to-make, authentic provincial recipes compiled by former head chef at New York's Fitz-Carlton Hotel: onion soup, lamb stew, potato pie, more. 309pp. 5⅜ x 8½. 23665-X Pa. $3.95

SAUCES, FRENCH AND FAMOUS, Louis Diat. Complete book gives over 200 specific recipes: bechamel, Bordelaise, hollandaise, Cumberland, apri-cot, etc. Author was one of this century's finest chefs, originator of vichyssoise and many other dishes. Index. 156pp. 5⅜ x 8. 23663-3 Pa. $2.75

TOLL HOUSE TRIED AND TRUE RECIPES, Ruth Graves Wakefield. Authentic recipes from the famous Mass. restaurant: popovers, veal and ham loaf, Toll House baked beans, chocolate cake crumb pudding, much more. Many helpful hints. Nearly 700 recipes. Index. 376pp. 5⅜ x 8½. 23560-2 Pa. $4.95

ILLUSTRATED GUIDE TO SHAKER FURNITURE, Robert Meader. Director, Shaker Museum, Old Chatham, presents up-to-date coverage of all furniture and appurtenances, with much on local styles not available elsewhere. 235 photos. 146pp. 9 x 12. 22819-3 Pa. $6.95

COOKING WITH BEER, Carole Fahy. Beer has as superb an effect on food as wine, and at fraction of cost. Over 250 recipes for appetizers, soups, main dishes, desserts, breads, etc. Index. 144pp. 5⅜ x 8½. (Available in U.S. only) 23661-7 Pa. $3.00

STEWS AND RAGOUTS, Kay Shaw Nelson. This international cookbook offers wide range of 108 recipes perfect for everyday, special occasions, meals-in-themselves, main dishes. Economical, nutritious, easy-to-prepare: goulash, Irish stew, boeuf bourguignon, etc. Index. 134pp. 5⅜ x 8½. 23662-5 Pa. $3.95

DELICIOUS MAIN COURSE DISHES, Marian Tracy. Main courses are the most important part of any meal. These 200 nutritious, economical recipes from around the world make every meal a delight. "I . . . have found it so useful in my own household,"—N.Y. Times. Index. 219pp. 5⅜ x 8½. 23664-1 Pa. $3.95

FIVE ACRES AND INDEPENDENCE, Maurice G. Kains. Great back-to-the-land classic explains basics of self-sufficient farming: economics, plants, crops, animals, orchards, soils, land selection, host of other necessary things. Do not confuse with skimpy faddist literature; Kains was one of America's greatest agriculturalists. 95 illustrations. 397pp. 5⅜ x 8½. 20974-1 Pa. $4.95

A PRACTICAL GUIDE FOR THE BEGINNING FARMER, Herbert Jacobs. Basic, extremely useful first book for anyone thinking about moving to the country and starting a farm. Simpler than Kains, with greater emphasis on country living in general. 246pp. 5⅜ x 8½. 23675-7 Pa. $3.95

PAPERMAKING, Dard Hunter. Definitive book on the subject by the foremost authority in the field. Chapters dealing with every aspect of history of craft in every part of the world. Over 320 illustrations. 2nd, revised and enlarged (1947) edition. 672pp. 5⅜ x 8½. 23619-6 Pa. $8.95

THE ART DECO STYLE, edited by Theodore Menten. Furniture, jewelry, metalwork, ceramics, fabrics, lighting fixtures, interior decors, exteriors, graphics from pure French sources. Best sampling around. Over 400 photographs. 183pp. 8⅜ x 11¼. 22824-X Pa. $6.95

ACKERMANN'S COSTUME PLATES, Rudolph Ackermann. Selection of 96 plates from the Repository of Arts, best published source of costume for English fashion during the early 19th century. 12 plates also in color. Captions, glossary and introduction by editor Stella Blum. Total of 120pp. 8⅜ x 11¼. 23690-0 Pa. $5.00

CATALOGUE OF DOVER BOOKS

THE ANATOMY OF THE HORSE, George Stubbs. Often considered the great masterpiece of animal anatomy. Full reproduction of 1766 edition, plus prospectus; original text and modernized text. 36 plates. Introduction by Eleanor Garvey. 121pp. 11 x 14¾. 23402-9 Pa. $8.95

BRIDGMAN'S LIFE DRAWING, George B. Bridgman. More than 500 illustrative drawings and text teach you to abstract the body into its major masses, use light and shade, proportion; as well as specific areas of anatomy, of which Bridgman is master. 192pp. 6½ x 9¼. (Available in U.S. only) 22710-3 Pa. $4.50

ART NOUVEAU DESIGNS IN COLOR, Alphonse Mucha, Maurice Verneuil, Georges Auriol. Full-color reproduction of *Combinaisons ornementales* (c. 1900) by Art Nouveau masters. Floral, animal, geometric, interlacings, swashes—borders, frames, spots—all incredibly beautiful. 60 plates, hundreds of designs. 9⅜ x 8-1/16. 22885-1 Pa. $4.50

FULL-COLOR FLORAL DESIGNS IN THE ART NOUVEAU STYLE, E. A. Seguy. 166 motifs, on 40 plates, from *Les fleurs et leurs applications decoratives* (1902): borders, circular designs, repeats, allovers, "spots." All in authentic Art Nouveau colors. 48pp. 9⅜ x 12¼. 23439-8 Pa. $6.00

A DIDEROT PICTORIAL ENCYCLOPEDIA OF TRADES AND INDUSTRY, edited by Charles C. Gillispie. 485 most interesting plates from the great French Encyclopedia of the 18th century show hundreds of working figures, artifacts, process, land and cityscapes; glassmaking, papermaking, metal extraction, construction, weaving, making furniture, clothing, wigs, dozens. of other activities. Plates fully explained. 920pp. 9 x 12. 22284-5, 22285-3 Clothbd., Two-vol. set $50.00

HANDBOOK OF EARLY ADVERTISING ART, Clarence P. Hornung. Largest collection of copyright-free early and antique advertising art ever compiled. Over 6,000 illustrations, from Franklin's time to the 1890's for special effects, novelty. Valuable source, almost inexhaustible.
Pictorial Volume. Agriculture, the zodiac, animals, autos, birds, Christmas, fire engines, flowers, trees, musical instruments, ships, games and sports, much more. Arranged by subject matter and use. 237 plates. 288pp. 9 x 12. 20122-8 Clothbd. $15.00

Typographical Volume. Roman and Gothic faces ranging from 10 point to 300 point, "Barnum," German and Old English faces, script, logotypes, scrolls and flourishes, 1115 ornamental initials, 67 complete alphabets, more. 310 plates. 320pp. 9 x 12. 20123-6 Clothbd. $15.00

CALLIGRAPHY (CALLIGRAPHIA LATINA), J. G. Schwandner. High point of 18th-century ornamental calligraphy. Very ornate initials, scrolls, borders, cherubs, birds, lettered examples. 172pp. 9 x 13. 20475-8 Pa. $7.95

GEOMETRY, RELATIVITY AND THE FOURTH DIMENSION, Rudolf Rucker. Exposition of fourth dimension, means of visualization, concepts of relativity as Flatland characters continue adventures. Popular, easily followed yet accurate, profound. 141 illustrations. 133pp. 5⅜ x 8½.
23400-2 Pa. $2.75

THE ORIGIN OF LIFE, A. I. Oparin. Modern classic in biochemistry, the first rigorous examination of possible evolution of life from nitrocarbon compounds. Non-technical, easily followed. Total of 295pp. 5⅜ x 8½.
60213-3 Pa. $5.95

PLANETS, STARS AND GALAXIES, A. E. Fanning. Comprehensive introductory survey: the sun, solar system, stars, galaxies, universe, cosmology; quasars, radio stars, etc. 24pp. of photographs. 189pp. 5⅜ x 8½. (Available in U.S. only)
21680-2 Pa. $3.75

THE THIRTEEN BOOKS OF EUCLID'S ELEMENTS, translated with introduction and commentary by Sir Thomas L. Heath. Definitive edition. Textual and linguistic. notes, mathematical analysis, 2500 years of critical commentary. Do not confuse with abridged school editions. Total of 1414pp. 5⅜ x 8½.
60088-2, 60089-0, 60090-4 Pa., Three-vol. set $19.50